The Mysteries

Rudolf Steiner's Writings on Spiritual Initiation

Selected and introduced by Andrew Welburn

The Protogonos or 'First Born' God of the Orphic Mysteries,
with symbols of Eternity and of the cosmic Totality.
Relief from Modena.

The Mysteries

Rudolf Steiner's Writings on Spiritual Initiation

Selected and introduced
by Andrew Welburn

Floris Books

First published by Floris Books in 1997
© 1997 Andrew Welburn

British Library CIP Data available

ISBN 0-86315-243-0

Printed in Great Britain
by Redwood Books, Trowbridge, Wilts.

Contents

Editor's foreword

The Mysteries in the ancient world were the source of secret wisdom and spiritual renewal — small wonder that they have been an object of fascination to modern times! Yet few have been able to cast any real light on the experiences of the initiates, or to open the doors of their temples to the world of today. One exception is the author of the writings gathered in this book.

Considerably before the rise of recent 'alternative' forms of thought, Rudolf Steiner, the Austrian philosopher and esotericist, issued his own challenge to the accepted ideas and values of the early twentieth century. It is perhaps only in retrospect, with an eye on the movements for individual freedom and ecological awareness that have come to a head in the intervening decades, that the greatness of his achievement begins to stand out. At the same time, to study his thought is to experience the shock of transition from the piecemeal wisdom acquired from the experience of modern times to a vision of human potential and spiritual wholeness whose scope still has the power to make us pause. If Steiner was right, we still have much rethinking to do.

That double perspective is, I think, evident in all the studies included in this book. It would be possible, on the one hand, to say much about the way Steiner's thought on many subjects strikingly anticipates the breakthroughs that have transformed our understanding. On the nature of myth, for example, Steiner's concern with structures and with the unconscious shaping forces behind images and beliefs already uses all that is best in modern structuralist interpretation. Even more important, however, is the realization which Steiner impresses upon us that such a breakthrough ought to have brought with it a deeper comprehension of religious truth. Durkheim's discovery of the social meaning of religion ought to have made those underlying psychic powers all the more real to us, more clearly rooted in the deeper experiences of personal and social renewal, which in ancient times were enacted in the Mysteries and nowadays struggle for expression in dream and obscure, sometimes violent, feelings. Instead, science and religion and the realities of social existence often remain contradictory in their demands upon the modern individual, who is left with only the meaninglessness of the immense pressures exerted upon him.

Or take Steiner's ideas about Plato. They bring us even closer to contemporary thought. Of course there have been in the interval many studies of Plato's attitude to the Mysteries — approving or ironic? Did he think them noble or fit for the vulgar? Yet no-one took up Steiner's insight that the Mysteries might take us inside the processes of Plato's philosophy itself. Recently Michael L. Morgan 'came to think that historians of philosophy should not forget historical context, and the idea occurred to me that Greek ecstatic ritual and mystery cults might provide a helpful vehicle for understanding Plato's thought ... ' (*Platonic Piety: Philosophy and Ritual in Fourth-Century Athens*, New Haven 1990, p.ix). And to get inside Plato's philosophy is to get inside philosophy itself in its historical origins, the setting of the scene for all of Western thought. Here again Steiner was far ahead: the concept of philosophy as an inner process leading to reorientation of the senses and the mind, an initiation in Mystery-terms, had already been there in his philosophical testament, *The Philosophy of Freedom*. Its message is one we can understand more forcefully in the era after Wittgenstein; but in this book Steiner shows that it is true also to the impulse that brought philosophy into being.

The present selection began as an attempt to translate Steiner's early work on Christianity and the Mysteries, *Das Christentum als mystische Tatsache*, and to add to it passages from his subsequent lectures and books in which he made further contributions to a theme that occupied him throughout his career. The end-product is both narrower and wider than that original notion. Much of the material still comes from that seminal work which announced Steiner's perspective, but I have selected chapters that show one major trajectory rather than the full range of his thinking. Steiner was an evolutionist, and throughout his writing we find an awareness of simultaneous continuity and metamorphosis. His stress lay on the permanent value of the Mystery-experience in its spiritual dimension, but also on the changing intellectual and religious meanings that it came to bear in the course of history. That is why, for example, he concentrates on the transitional figures of the early philosophers, the pre-Socratics. At first it might seem eccentric to focus a case for their connection with the Mysteries on Heraclitus and Pythagoras (see Chapter 3) rather than, say, the 'divine' Empedocles; but it is part of Steiner's point that rational thinking did not come into being by banishing a superstitious, 'fanciful' mentality of early man, it was a transformation of Mystery-ideas. Steiner made that point again in his later study of Pherecydes of Syros, who fascinated him by his involvement in the very moment of the 'birth of thinking.' I have added it to the earlier work because he also shows how the step into rationality was not in fact a step away from the Mysteries at all, but a deepening of the Mystery.

Something similar applies to Chapter 6 on 'the Christian Mystery,' the Apocalypse of John. One aspect of the deepening Mystery is the emergence of the individual, and it is in Christianity that the individual is given spiritual significance. That is one reason why Steiner was concerned that revival of interest in the Mysteries should not take an anti-Christian direction. (The fact that the Christian Churches seemed largely to have brought that hostility upon themselves was, and remains, one of the ironies of the case.) Just as reason was not a banishing of primitive mentality but a transformation, a metamorphosis of the soul, individuality need not be a denial of the cosmic meaning of human existence. And the Mysteries were once again the clue to the continuity. In the

Apocalypse, individual existence and cosmic drama are indissolubly bound up together, the ordeals of initiation and the release of the images of vision are translated into facts of history in the universal Mystery, the initiation of all mankind. In the wake of modern discoveries such as the Gnostic writings from Nag Hammadi, and the Essene scriptures of the 'Dead Sea Scrolls,' we can no longer close our eyes to the visionary side of early Christianity, suppressed by the later Church. Steiner's view of the continuity between the Mysteries and Christianity again anticipates many contemporary rethinkings about Christian origins. But it is the Apocalypse that, accepted into the Church's canon after many misgivings, kept alive the Mystery-dimension of Christianity, and it rightly occupies centre-stage in the presentation below. I have enriched Steiner's short original chapter with readings from his expansive lectures. In these once more he challenges the modern religious historian's conclusion 'that Christianity triumphed in the world and became a universal religion only because it detached itself from the climate of the Greco-Oriental mysteries and proclaimed itself a religion of salvation accessible to all' (M. Eliade, *Rites and Symbols of Initiation*, New York 1965, p.*ix*). Christianity was a further stage, not a discarding of the Mysteries. Likewise the idea that the Mysteries can be renewed only by rejecting our Christian inheritance is seen to be in truth succumbing to a false dichotomy, if one rooted in the perspective wrongly imposed originally by the Church itself.

The result is a series of interlocking studies that I hope reveal something of the depth and relevance of Steiner's thought today. Behind them all stands his profound understanding of the human spirit, and his evolutionary picture of human origins and destiny that is so unlike Darwin's. All evolutionary advance is necessarily the breaking-up, the dissolution of an earlier harmony — a process in which there is loss as well as gain, sacrifice or renunciation as well as victory over circumstance. Steiner's philosophy attempts to do justice to this spiritual–moral aspect of evolution, and it seemed to him that the ancient mythologies of the Fall were, in their pictorial fashion, more keenly evolutionary in their imaginative implications than the notions of continuously advancing progress with which science optimistically but uncritically tended to align itself. But all of us experience these things whenever we advance to a new stage of maturity, or wrestle our way to an understanding of existential facts. Steiner constantly refers us to the inner processes of our hidden life, which the Mysteries needed to do no more than raise into the life of picture and idea, drama and historical event. It is to the awareness of our humanity that Steiner constantly points, in the conviction that it contains the key to our own evolution and that of the world in which we live.

The notes that I have added are intended to serve a variety of purposes, but all of them may be summarized as an attempt to bridge the gap between the situation in which Steiner wrote (or spoke) and our own. It is well known, for example, that there have been a significant number of discoveries relating to the origins of Christianity: the 'Dead Sea Scrolls,' which reveal the esoteric background within Judaism to the world of the Gospels; the Nag Hammadi Library of Gnostic writings from the early Christian centuries just mentioned. But perhaps the most disturbing aspect of those novel texts has not so much been to reveal a hitherto unknown landscape, as to show us the well-known documents from the New Testament in the milieu that gave rise to them, an esoteric and (by later standards) unorthodox welter of ideas. Only gradually did the Church select the documents it wished to preserve, detaching them from the urgent, experimental thought of the first Christians in their struggle to comprehend Christ. The excitement of the new discoveries should therefore not be played off against Steiner's concentration on the previously known Gospels and Revelation (the Apocalypse). What is so staggering is the way that Steiner already showed us the spiritual background to early Christianity that the Scrolls and the Gnostic Gospels have now made undeniable. It is possible to conceive ways of engineering more directly a synthesis of the new texts and Steiner's descriptions — but that would be a different book.

In other cases, too, the lack of direct supporting evidence meant that Steiner had to go around a problem. The content of the Greek Mysteries, for instance, is recorded by none of the classical authors — precisely because it was a holy secret. He had to point to traces of their content where it could be found, if somewhat transformed, in the early philosophers. In this domain too, however, there have been fortunate discoveries. One, the papyrus from Derveni, preserves a sacred text intended to be burnt on the funeral pyre of an Orphic initiate. Evidently it rolled out of the flames and survived, only slightly charred. Together with such remarkable objects as the 'gold plates' and the membership tokens of a Dionysus-cult, it has helped us grasp directly, if still inadequately, the nature of Orphic mysteriosophy. It has also revealed precisely the sort of links with pre-Socratic philosophy that Steiner indicated. Once again, new materials have made Steiner's approach, even where it had to be indirect, not less relevant, but more.

Beyond the interpreting of detailed evidence, Steiner's description is valuable for its account of the changing, evolving human consciousness that underlies the various forms of religious life. What he meant by esotericism reflects his understanding that new awareness has to be pioneered by those with a special calling, and with a training that will enable them to bear the burdens as well as the insights of 'higher knowledge.' Christianity has brought this spiritual individualization-process, formerly the province of the few in the Mysteries, increasingly into the lives of people everywhere. Indeed, that emergence of the creative individual, even when it takes place in a setting that appears secularized or psychological, personal, is an aspect of what Steiner meant by the Christ-impulse, working in us in an evolutionary sense. The initiation of all mankind foretold in the Apocalypse is everyday experience for many in the modern world.

That is the real reason why it is so important for us to understand what is going on, and to catch up in ideas with the forces that are actually shaping us if we are not to fail the initiatory trials. The Mystery-dimension is what Steiner restored to our perception of Christianity, and in the concluding lecture he speaks more explicitly of the 'cosmic Christ' and what he can mean to us today.

It is my hope that, as a result, this book may serve as a valid introduction to Steiner's presentation of Christianity, not just as an historical process, but as a power that can bring new awareness of the kind needed so desperately if we are to solve the ecological and human problems that face us. Steiner spoke of that awareness becoming a consciousness of the presence of Christ, in a wholly modern, individual way: the reality, as he described it, of the prophecies of the *parousia*, the 'second coming.' Here again, it would be quite wrong to contrast this 'visionary' aspect with 'historical Christianity.' What Steiner shows again and again is that by really understanding our past we can move freely forward into the future.

Some special terms that recur in the pages below may usefully be defined:

— *mystes* (fem. *mystis*, pl. *mystai)*, an initiate in the Mysteries, one who had been through the secret rites and had experience of the divine powers and knowledge that they communicated;

— mysteriosophy, the teaching of the Mysteries; whereas most of the older Mysteries took a fundamentally ritual form, in some there was an increasing body of written and oral teaching (e.g. in Orphism, Mithraism and the Gnostic cults);

— initiand, the one-to-be-initiated, neophyte;

— *daimon*, a divine or semi-divine being; some of the early philosophers taught that we have such a being, or the

potential of one, within us; later the term came into
disrepute: for the Church all such divine beings were
anathema, as they were not the one true God, and the
word gradually turned into our 'demon'; originally,
however, the word had no evil connotation.

All titles and subtitles are editorial; full references to sources
are given in each place. Footnotes marked with symbols are
'asides' in Steiner's text best presented as notes on the page;
numbered endnotes are the editor's, and when Steiner is
quoted within them it is in the third person and within
quotation marks. References are normally given to available
editions and translations.

Sometimes, for example, in his *Apocalypse* lectures, Steiner
seemed to take it for granted that his auditors had been
recently perusing the text and would be able to follow his
detailed remarks. A reader is in a somewhat different situation; hence I have occasionally inserted a further passage of
quotation, identified in the note that refers to it.

Steiner's digression on *The Odyssey* (in Chapter 1 here)
seemed so substantial, and concerned for the only time in
that discussion with a literary text rather than oral myth and
the images employed in the traditional tales, that I have
taken the liberty of appending it to the chapter.

The italicized editorial paragraphs introducing each chapter
are not meant to summarize their content but to help orientate the reader in current issues to which they seem relevant.

Finally it should be noted that the grammatical use of 'he'
or 'man,' and so on, when referring to general or indefinite
numbers of persons should not be taken to exclude the
significant participation of women either in the Mysteries or
in the life of Christianity.

Andrew Welburn
New College, Oxford
Christmas 1996

1. The Dying God

Interpretations of the ancient Mysteries are inevitably coloured by modern concerns. Students of their religious meaning have been troubled in particular by the problem of their relationship to Christianity, which is often striking but not very easy to interpret. The similarity has sometimes been used to attack the claims of Christianity to a unique revelation; others have sought to minimize the issue by arguing that elements of Mystery language and ritual in early Christianity were merely outer vestiges belonging to its time, from which it soon freed itself. More recently, however, the discoveries of Gnostic and other early Christian works have made all such sweepingly simple solutions seem inadequate. In the situation that has resulted, Rudolf Steiner's bold facing of the issues still has much to teach us: he is determined to get away from the strategy of scoring points, and to understand more deeply the nature both of the Mysteries and of the Christian claim. By elucidating the spiritual purpose and direction of each he manages to show the changing spiritual needs and the underlying continuities of mankind's religious experience. On that foundation he also challenges some of the assumptions of, for instance, Darwinistic science which ignores the moral dimension of life. But he challenges it on its own ground, not by offering a 'fundamentalist' alternative, and further scientific thought (mentioned in the notes) has tended to confirm his ideas in a way that offers to clarify the real meaning of death — and the resurrection.

From: *Bausteine zu einer Erkenntnis des Mysteriums von Golgatha* (lectures, 1917; GA no. 175). Extracts from lecture 2.

That the human soul can find the path to the spirit was never doubted throughout the ages of mankind's primitive history. It was beyond doubt, too, that in his life between birth and death the spirit was a living presence in the human soul, which thereby participated in the divine life. This conviction was founded on the immediate awareness of the spirit which underlay the cults and practices of the Mysteries.[1] (It is also worth noting that one of the earliest Greek philosophers, Heraclitus, already speaks of the Mysteries as having possessed enormous importance for humanity in times long gone by, though they have now passed the zenith of their influence. Thus quite early on — sixth century BC — enlightened Greeks already spoke of a decline of the Mysteries.)[2]

The practices of the Mysteries were extremely varied; but we are concerned here only with the central idea — the central idea of the Mysteries as they were practised on into the Christian era and up to the time of the Emperor Julian, 'the Apostate.' It is worth pausing to consider this central idea, partly because recent discussion of the Mysteries has assumed a somewhat anti-Christian tenor. For it has been pointed out that what we know as the Easter story, the Mystery of Golgotha — in effect the story of Christ's passion and death which is absolutely central to Christianity — was universally known in the Mysteries. And the conclusion is drawn that the Easter mystery of Christianity is nothing more than pagan myth and ritual taken over from the Mysteries and applied to the person of Jesus of Nazareth.[3] Indeed, for many the case appears so overwhelming that any further doubt is impossible. In their view, when Christians assert that in Christ God suffered, was put to death and rose again, and by his resurrection gave promise of hope and salvation to men, they are expressing as Christian ideas things which were to be found in various forms in the Mystery-cults. Pagan myths and rites are collected together and fused into the Easter story by being applied to the figure of Jesus of Nazareth

Most recently there has been a further development, which

is the more remarkable in that it has come from the circles of official Christianity (I think especially of certain movements afoot in Bremen). According to this, the evidence for the historical Jesus must be regarded as extremely ambivalent, to say the least.[4] What happened was rather that in the life of the community various features drawn from the mythology and the rites of the Mysteries came together and assumed a single 'centralized' form — a process which led to the formation within primitive Christianity of the 'myth of Christ' out of the ancient pagan myths. There was a discussion in Berlin a few years ago,* where it emerged that we have no way of knowing about a historical Jesus of Nazareth, only about the idea of Christ which arose as a result of diverse social forces in the primitive Christian church.

The comparative study of the Mystery-cults and Christianity opens the door to endless temptations. To illustrate the background of the Easter mystery, we may take the case of a cultic festival in Phrygia, of which we have an authentic description. It is just one example of a widespread type of festival. The description comes from the work of Firmicus Maternus, addressed to the sons of Constantine. He tells us how the statue of Attis — or at least of some divinity, whose exact identity need not concern us just now — was carried round in a midnight ritual procession, bound to the trunk of a tree. The sufferings of the god were then celebrated, and in that connection a 'lamb' was placed at the foot of the tree:

> On a certain night a statue is laid flat on its back on a bier, where it is bemoaned in cadenced plaints. Then when the worshippers have had their fill of ... lamentation, a light is brought in. Next a priest anoints the throats of all who were mourning, and once that is done he whispers in a low murmur:

* Though it took place only a few years ago, the terrible events of the War have made it seem frighteningly remote from the present, and in many ways given the discussion the character of a mythical happening!

> Take comfort, *mystai*, for the god is saved, you also
> will find salvation from all your needs ... So you
> should die as he dies, and you should live as he lives.[5]

The resurrection of the god was proclaimed with the break-
ing day. The previous day, when the god was bound to the
tree and so symbolically given over to death, there had been
ritual lamentation and terrible wailing. Now, when next day
the resurrection of the god was celebrated, the lament was
suddenly transformed into wild outbursts of joy.

Firmicus also tells us that the statue of the god was buried
in another location. While the lamentation was at its height
during the nocturnal vigil, a light suddenly shone in the
darkness. The grave was opened. The god had risen from the
dead. The priest then spoke the words:

> Take comfort, *mystai*, for the god is saved, you also
> will find salvation from all your needs.

Thus these rituals, which were celebrated over many centuries prior to the Mystery of Golgotha, bear an undeniable
resemblance to the Easter mystery which came to be known
within Christianity. That is why the hypothesis of a 'central-
izing' around Jesus of Nazareth of ideas concerning a
suffering, dying and rising god by the early Christians is so
seductive.

It is important to understand the real origin of the pre-
Christian, pagan rites. They have their roots far back in the
time when the Mysteries developed out of a profound vision
of man and his connection with the cosmos, as it was
perceived in atavistic clairvoyant states.[6] Of course, by the
time of the Phrygian festival described above the authentic
meaning of these things was not necessarily grasped — any
more than the modern Freemasons always understand what
happens in their ceremonies. Nevertheless, the Mysteries look
back to what was originally a grandiose knowledge of the
place of man in the cosmos, though it is a kind of knowledge

that is hard to convey in modern terms. For consider: man is embedded in his setting and depends upon it, not just in physical terms but in living connection through his soul and spirit. It is an environment also of ideas and concepts on which he draws, forming his assumptions and habits of thought. Hence with the best will in the world it is difficult to escape from these perspectives and understand the type of experiences which are no longer — for reasons connected with the whole spiritual evolution of mankind — those of modern humanity. ...

At the heart of the consciousness that, in hidden ways, underlies the archaic Mysteries (including the Mysteries of Attis that we have discussed) is the sense that man is not born for death — and yet he dies. That was what the Mysteries sought to articulate. It was the enigma to which they provided an answer.

Why were the Mysteries celebrated? The celebrations took place so that people should be reminded, every year, of something that they wished to make a reality for the soul. They wished to be reassured that the time had not yet come when they would have to confront in all seriousness the inexplicable fact of death. The adherents of the Attis-cult had the instinctive sense that a time was coming on earth when the inexplicable reality of death would confront them in utter seriousness. But it was not yet. And inasmuch as the priests celebrated the passion and resurrection of the god, the Mystery-rites offered the consoling knowledge that the time had not yet come when they had to face without flinching the fact of death.

Now by all means let us call the event described in the opening chapters of the Old Testament a 'symbol.' But the reality behind the symbol was everywhere acknowledged in Antiquity. Ancient humanity instinctively understood what was meant by 'Luciferic temptation.'[7] It is in fact modern materialism which has for the first time lost the instinctive sense of the reality which it connotes. The materialistic theory of Darwin has led to a kind of intellectual perversity which is scarcely calculated to lead to the truth in this domain. For it supposes that over a long period of time, certain sorts of animal gradually turned into present-day man. In the perspective of Darwinism, therefore, there is no place for anything corresponding to the 'temptation' or the 'fall from Paradise.' We can hardly suppose that Lucifer tempted an ape-Adam or an ape-Eve.[8]

However, in times past there was still an instinctive appreciation of certain specific facts, which are clothed in narrative form in the early passages of the Old Testament story. They looked at these facts in more or less the following way. The archetypal form of physical man contained in its organization, so they said, nothing of mortality. Certain facts show, on the other hand, that something has infected man's archetypal form with the tendency to corruption — show in fact that there is within his organization a principle of death. The process of man's becoming subject to death was connected with his capacity for moral action, as is indicated — and I shall return to the implications of this later — in the enigmatic phrase 'original sin.' Man's mortality is not simply the result of his being subject to the laws of nature which apply to every material being, but has a moral dimension. Man's mortality has its roots in the soul.[9]

An animal does not have an individual soul; its soul-identity is the species, and as such it does not die. It is embodied in particular animals, each of which is mortal in so far as it is a physical organism. But the soul of the species relinquishes the dying animal and remains just as it was before it was embodied there. The particular animal organism inevitably dies. The human organism is a rather different case. For in the case of human beings, the collective identity of humankind or soul of the species is uniquely expressed in each individual, and gives to each, simply as an outer expression of the human organization, immortality. If man nevertheless becomes mortal, it can only be as a result of an act of his own soul, a moral act. In a certain way man can only experience mortality as something brought about by his own soul. This is a concrete experience — there is no use in substituting the kind of abstract formulations so often sought today in these domains.

Certainly in ancient times, up to the centuries before the Mystery of Golgotha while the Mysteries were still celebrated, the soul was experienced as the source of human mortality with utter intensity. The human soul had fallen away in the course of time into corruption, into ever increasing corruption of the organism by the soul which had become a principle of destruction to the organism. Ancient humanity looked back to a moral event, which meant that simply by coming into a body at birth, the soul had become an agent of destruction to the body. And because of this, the life it lived between the birth and death could no longer be in a state of 'incorruption.' Over centuries and indeed over millennia, this situation became worse and worse. Ancient humanity felt that the soul was more and more an agent of destruction to the body, and was less and less able to find the way back to the spiritual world of human development, the soul only sows the seeds of death in the body which has become increasingly corrupt. And a time must therefore come when souls will no longer be able to find their way back at all to the spiritual world after their time on earth.

This moment was awaited in the ancient world with fear and trembling. People said to each other that, in generations to come, the soul would ultimately so corrupt the body and sow the seeds of death that humanity would no longer be able to find the way back to God; that time must come. They wished to know, however, whether that time was drawing near or was still some way off, and this was the function of the Attis-cults and similar rites.[10] They were an attempt to discover whether the souls of men still had enough of the divine within them that the moment had not yet come — the moment when souls should have lost all their divine heritage and no longer be able to find their way again to God. That is why the words of the priest were charged with such a depth of meaning:

Take comfort, *mystai,* for the god is saved, you also
will find salvation from all your needs.

The priest meant that God is still active in the world, that the
souls of men had not yet severed all connection with the
divine. The god has overcome death once again.[11] He wished
to comfort the people by this proclamation of the god who
was still within them.

We touch here upon unplumbed depths of emotion and
complexes of feeling characteristic of those times in human
history. Modern man has focussed his attention so much on
the external world that he no longer has any inkling of the
inner struggles which people underwent. They may have
been people lacking in everything we now call 'culture' —
they had not even the art of writing — but they had depths
of feeling. In the priestly schools, which preserved the last
vestiges of the tradition stemming from the archaic clairvoyant vision, they expressed these feelings by saying that if
things went forward under the impact of 'the Fall,' there
would ultimately be no alternative: souls would turn away
from God to a world of death. It would be a world of their
own making, in so far as they have progressively sown the
seeds of death and corruption in the human body. It would
be a shackling of the soul to the earth, or one could even say
a descent into the underworld. It would be the death of the
soul. That is not to say, of course, that man's spirit — his
eternally existent and autonomous self — would be lost. The
distinction between the body, soul and spirit of man was
preserved in these schools of mysteriosophy. But the soul-
nature would be lost, never to return.* The spirits of men
would be embodied in a soulless, inert condition — not in

* The spirit was acknowledged as the eternally reappearing nature of
man in all his earthly lives, whereas souls might well fall into the
underworld and be lost. And a future period of the earth's development
might be one in which human spirits would be embodied once more, but
in which they would look back on the soul as lost forever from the life
of the earth.

the living way that movement and gesture are experienced as expressions of the living soul.

What, on the other hand, was the feeling which drew Christians to the Easter mystery? It was the feeling that unless something new entered earthly life, man would in future be embodied as a creature without a soul — therefore they must await something new! They were waiting for something that could not come from the life of the earth but had to come into it from outside. And they found what they were waiting for in the Mystery of Golgotha.

It was necessary that a Being should enter into existence on the earth so as to rescue the soul and snatch it from the jaws of death (I speak now of the soul, not of the spirit, as needing to be snatched from the jaws of death). They recognized that in the body of Jesus of Nazareth a Being entered into earthly becoming, appearing as the Christ to redeem men's souls. Through an inner union with the Christ, the soul of man puts off its tendency to corrupt the body. All that had been lost could gradually be restored. Thus the Mystery of Golgotha stands at the central point of earthly history. From the beginning of earthly creation until the Mystery of Golgotha there had been a progressive decline and the forces of corruption had increasingly invaded man's soul, so that he would have become a soulless automaton. From the Mystery of Golgotha until the end of the earth comes the time of renewal when all that had been lost would be gathered together once more, so that when earthly history comes to its end the spirits of men would once again be embodied in immortal forms. Human bodies would once again be immortal — that was the expectation underlying the Easter mystery.[12] Before it could come about, however, it was necessary to conquer the power which had caused the moral corruption of the soul. And that is what, according to Christianity, took place in the decisive historical event of Golgotha.

2. The Mysteries and their Myths

The wisdom of the Mysteries was expressed, not exactly in philosophical teachings but in myths — stories handed down by oral tradition, and later sometimes in written form. These myths are a source of endless fascination to many people today, but few have been able to bring us closer to understanding the consciousness of those to whom they were originally entrusted as divine revelations. Recent study of the significance of myths for primitive and archaic societies has taken a leap forward through the use of 'structural' analysis, leading beyond the literal content of the story to the underlying patterns of thought and values in a culture. Rudolf Steiner already adopted an approach which threw the emphasis on to structure as a revelation of the spiritual processes that lay behind the myth, though he rightly resisted the notion that religious values are merely an expression of their time. Rather, through their initiation the mystai *reveal how the moral and intellectual forms of a culture are forged, and the myths dramatize the creative patterns which make social and religious life possible. Although he gives ample scope for the psychological exploration of myth, therefore, Steiner's interpretation moves beyond the merely inward meaning of the mythic structures to see them as spiritual discoveries with an objective social reality. In the great festivals which were the outer accompaniment of the initiatory rites, for example at Eleusis near Athens, he sees the creation of forms of life that are touched by the initiates' consciousness of the eternal, their own immortal part, expressing a cosmic process of rebirth. Some of his subsequent indications concerning details of the cult-statues have been borne out by archaeological discovery in Sicily and elsewhere.*

From: *Das Christentum als mystische Tatsache* (original edition 1902; GA no. 8). Complete translation of the section *'Die Mysterienweisheit und der Mythos.'*

The structures of myth

The powers and beings which the initiates in the ancient Mysteries sought to find within themselves remain unknown to anyone whose horizon is bounded by received ideas. For the *mystai* did not hold back from the great question. They enquired into their own spiritual nature, and into powers and laws beyond those of lower, natural existence.

In his ordinary life of thought, based on the senses and what may be inferred from them, man worships gods of his own making,[1] or — when he finds this out — is driven to disclaim them. The *mystai*, however, are aware of their god-making; and they understand the reasons why they do so. They have won through, as we should say, to the underlying laws which govern the process of making gods.[2] It is rather as if a plant were suddenly to become aware of the laws which determine its own growth and development. Up to now it has developed in serene unconsciousness, but once it knows the laws of its own being it necessarily changes fundamentally its whole relationship to itself. The poet's celebration of the plant-world, the scientist's investigation of botanical principles would now come before it as a conscious ideal. Such is the case of the *mystes* in his own sphere, with regard to the laws and the forces active within him. He has attained a *gnosis*, and consciously creates something divine, something beyond himself.

The initiates looked upon the well-known gods and myths, created by the people as an activity transcending the given world of nature, in the same way. They aspired to understand the laws governing the world of gods and myths. Where they found the figure of some divinity worshipped by the people, or a myth being told, they looked for a higher truth. Let us take an example.

The Athenians had been forced by King Minos of Crete to deliver up to him every eight years seven boys and seven maidens. These were thrown to the Minotaur — a horrible monster — to be devoured. When it came to the third time for the mournful tribute to be paid, Theseus, the king's son, went with it to Crete. On his arrival in Crete, King Minos' daughter Ariadne came to his aid. The Minotaur was kept in the Labyrinth — a maze from which no-one who entered it could ever find the way out. Now Theseus wished to deliver his native city from such a shameful tribute, and so had to be cast into the Labyrinth as if to become the monster's prey, and then kill the Minotaur. This task he undertook, overcame the formidable enemy, and then regained the open air. For Ariadne had given him a ball of thread to help him.[3]

The *mystai* wanted to understand how the creative human mind came to invent such a story. They studied the creative spirit in order to understand it, rather as a botanist studies plants. They were looking for the truth, an implicit wisdom, in what the myth expressed in popular form. Sallust adopts the standpoint of the Mysteries when he characterizes 'myth' in such terms:

> The universe itself can be called a myth, since bodies and material objects are apparent in it, while souls and intellects are concealed. Furthermore, to wish to teach all men the truth about the gods causes the foolish to despise, because they cannot learn, and the good to be slothful; whereas to conceal the truth by myths prevents the former from despising philosophy and compels the latter to study it.[4]

The *mystai* were aware of adding something to the myth which did not exist in the consciousness of the ordinary people when they sought for its 'implicit truth.' They placed themselves in the position of the scientist studying a plant. They were putting into words something totally foreign to the mythological consciousness — yet they looked upon it as the deeper truth, expressed in symbols through the myth: thus man confronts his own sensual nature as though it were a fierce monster; the fruits of his personal development fall as sacrifices to it, and it continues to devour them until the hero, the conqueror (Theseus) awakens in man. And it is through knowledge that he is able to slay the enemy — spinning the thread by means of which he finds the way out of the labyrinth of his sensual nature. Human knowledge itself is the Mystery expressed in this story of the conquering of sensuality. This is the 'secret' known to the *mystai*.

The Mystery-interpretation points to a psychological power in man. It is not a power of which we are normally aware; nevertheless it is active within us, generating the myth. And the myth has the same structure as the truth of the Mysteries.[5] It is in this way that the truth finds its symbol in the myth.

What, then, do we find in myths? They are the expression of a creative spirit, of the unconscious activity of the soul. The soul's creative work is determined by specific laws: it must be active in a particular way if it is to create something with a meaning beyond itself. On the mythological level it works with images. But the way these images are structured follows psychological laws. Hence one could add that when the soul develops beyond the mythological stage of consciousness to deeper forms of truth, these nevertheless bear the imprint of the same power which generated the myths.

The relationship between mythical imagery as a form of representation and higher, philosophical knowledge is thus stated by Plotinus from the standpoint of the Neoplatonic school, in connection with the guardians of priestly wisdom in Egypt:

> Whether as a result of rigorous investigations, or
> instinctively, in imparting their wisdom the wise men
> of the Egyptians do not expound their teaching and
> precepts by means of written signs, which are
> imitations of voice and speech. Instead they draw
> pictures; and in their temple engravings they illustrate
> the thought that goes with each particular thing, so
> that every picture is an object which embodies

knowledge and wisdom as a totality, without any analysis or discussion. Only afterwards is the content of the picture elicited verbally, and it is explained why it is so and not otherwise.[6]

The best place to examine the relation of mythical narratives to the nature of the Mysteries is in the outlook of those thinkers who acknowledged a harmony between their way of representing the world and the Mystery-process. That harmony is most fully documented in the case of Plato.

From myth to philosophy

Plato's interpretation of myths, and use of them in his teaching, may be regarded as a model case. Thus in the *Phaedrus*, or dialogue on the nature of the soul, we are introduced to the myth of Boreas. This is the god whose presence was felt in the blustering north wind. He caught sight one day of the beautiful Oreithyia, who was the daughter of Erechtheus, king of Attica, as she was out plucking flowers with her playmates. He was seized with love for her, carried her off and brought her to his cave. Through his mouthpiece in the dialogue, Socrates, Plato rejects the purely rationalistic interpretation of the myth, according to which the story is a poetic expression of purely natural, physical happenings — the stormwind caught the princess and blew her over the cliff. Socrates comments:

> Such explanations are too ingenious and laboured, it seems to me, and I don't altogether envy the man who devotes himself to this sort of work, if only because, when he has finished with Oreithyia, he must go on to put into proper shape ... all the other such monsters of mythology. ... A sceptic who proposes to force each one of them into a plausible shape with the aid of a sort of rough ingenuity will need a great deal of

leisure. ... So I let these things alone and acquiesce in the popular attitude towards them; as I've already said I make myself rather than them the object of my investigations, and I try to discover whether I am a more complicated and puffed-up sort of creature than Typhon or whether I am a more gentle and simpler creature, endowed by heaven with a nature altogether less typhonic.[7]

Thus we see that Plato is no enthusiast for the intellectual and rationalistic interpretation of myth, and this must be taken into account when we examine his own use of myths to express his own views.

Plato has recourse to myth when he comes to speak of the life of the soul. At that juncture, where he leaves the transitory world to seek after the eternal core of the soul, concepts deriving from the senses and from the thinking based upon them no longer apply. The *Phaedrus* is devoted to the theme of the eternal in the soul, and the soul is described as a chariot with two horses, each many-winged, and a charioteer.[8] One of the horses is docile and intelligent, the other headstrong and wild. When the chariot meets with an obstacle on its path, the headstrong beast seizes the chance of impeding the reliable one and defying the charioteer. And when the chariot reaches the point of ascending in the wake of the gods up the celestial steep, the intractable horse throws it into confusion. Whether the chariot can surmount these difficulties and attain to the realm of the supersensible depends on their relative strengths and so whether the good horse can gain the mastery. But the soul can never raise itself to the divine without some sort of a struggle. Some souls rise higher in their pursuit of the eternal vision, others less high.

Those souls which have attained the transcendent vision are kept safe until the next cycle, while those who have seen nothing but were thwarted by the unruly horse must enter upon a new cycle and try again. The cycles here designate the several incarnations of the soul, one cycle standing for its life as a particular personality. The unruly horse and the intelligent horse stand for the lower and the higher nature of man; the charioteer for the soul which aspires to 'diviniza-tion' as in the Mysteries. Plato appeals to the power of myth when he wants to describe the course of the eternal soul through its manifold transformations. And elsewhere in the platonic canon myth is used in order to render intelligible through symbolic stories the non-sensory, inner reality of man's being.*

In the light of this principle it is worth considering the Egyptian Mystery of Osiris.

In Osiris we have a figure who gradually became one of the most important gods of Egypt, supplanting the local cults in several parts of the country.[9] A significant cycle of myths grew up concerning Osiris and his consort, Isis. According to the story, Osiris was the son of the Sun-god; he had a bro-ther, Typhon (Set), and a sister, Isis. Osiris married his sister and with her reigned over Egypt. But his wicked brother

---

* This use of myth and parable by Plato can be paralleled in other contexts. For example, in the literature of ancient India there is a parable attributed to Buddha: there was a man who was passionately attached to life, and was on no account willing to die, who found himself pursued by four serpents. He heard a voice warning him to feed and bathe the serpents from time to time, but the man ran away in fear of the serpents. Again he heard a voice, warning him that he was being chased by five murderers; again he ran away. A voice told him of a sixth murderer who was about to cut off his head with a sword; once more he took to flight. He came to a deserted village. He heard a voice telling him that thieves were about to raid the village, and again he took to flight. He came to a great river. Feeling unsafe on this side of it, he made a basket out of straw, twigs and leaves and in it crossed to the far shore. Now he is safe — now he is a Brahman. The parable is interpreted as follows: a man must pass through the most various states on his way to the divine. The four serpents signify the four elements (fire, water, earth and air); the five murderers are the five senses. The deserted village stands for a soul which has freed itself from the impressions of the senses, but which is not yet secure within itself. If it takes hold inwardly of the lower nature alone, it will inevitably be destroyed. The man must assemble a boat which will take him from the shore of sense-perceptible nature across the river of transience to the other shore, that of eternity and the divine.

Typhon plotted to overthrow Osiris and prepared a chest which was exactly the length of Osiris' body. The chest was presented as a gift at a banquet to whatever person it fitted exactly: this turned out to be none other than Osiris, who lay down in the chest. Immediately Typhon and his confederates seized upon Osiris, closed the chest and threw it into the river. When Isis heard the terrible news, she wandered in despair searching for her husband's body. But when she found it, Typhon again managed to take possession of it: he tore it into fourteen pieces which were dispersed in different locations — several 'tombs of Osiris' were shown in Egypt. The limbs of the god were thus to be found scattered here and there in widely separated places. Osiris himself, however, came forth from the netherworld and vanquished Typhon. A ray from him fell upon Isis, who in consequence bore his son, Harpocrates (Horus).

And now compare with the myth the world-view presented by the fifth century BC Greek philosopher Empedocles. He asserted that an original unity was torn apart into the four elements (fire, water, earth and air) or into the multiplicity of existent beings. He posited two opposing powers which bring about within the world of existing things the processes of becoming and passing-away, namely Love and Strife. Empedocles says of the elements:

> They remain forever the same, yet mingling each other
>   with the others
> Become transformed into men and numberless
>   creatures besides them.
> Now they are joined into one, Love binding the many
>   together,
> Now they are scattered once more, dispersed through
>   hatred and Strife.[10]

From the Empedoclean standpoint, everything in the universe is simply the elements in different combinations. Things could only come into existence because the primal unity was torn apart into these four natures, dispersed into the elements of the cosmos. Hence if we encounter something, it is a constituent part of the scattered divinity. But the divinity is hidden in things as we see them; it had to perish in order for things to come into existence. For what are things but combinations of the members of God, organized into wholes by Love and Strife? In the words of Empedocles:

> See, for a clear demonstration, how the limbs of a man
> are constructed,
> All that the body possesses, in beauty and pride of
> existence,
> Brought together by Love, the elements forming a
> union.
> Then come hatred and Strife, and fatally tear them
> asunder,
> Once more they wander alone, on the desolate
> confines of life.
> So is it with the bushes, and trees, and the water-
> inhabiting fishes,
> Animals roaming the mountains, sea-birds borne by
> their wings.[11]

Empedocles clearly implies that the philosopher is one who rediscovers the divine original unity in things, hidden under a spell, whirled about by Love and Strife. But if man finds the divinity who is hidden there, he must himself be a divine being. For Empedocles adheres to the view that 'like can only be known by like.'[12,*]

These ideas about the nature of man and the cosmos

---

* An epistemological doctrine given expression in Goethe's saying:
  Wär nicht das Auge sonnenhaft,
  Wie könnten wir das Licht erblicken?
  Lebt nicht in uns des Gottes eigene Kraft,
  Wie könnt uns Göttliches entzücken?
'If the eye were not of the nature of the sun, how could we behold the light? If God's own power were not at work in us, how could divine things delight us?' (*Zahme Xenien*).

transcend considerations of sense-experience. They are ideas which the *mystai* found in their myth of Osiris: the god, the creative power, is poured out into the world. This appears in Empedocles' four elements. God — Osiris — is slain. Man, with his knowledge (which is divine in nature) will restore him to life. He is to rediscover him in the form of Horus (Son of God, wisdom) in the opposition between Strife (Typhon) and Love (Isis). In a Greek way Empedocles expresses his basic ideas in terms which still have a mythical ring: his Love is the goddess Aphrodite, his Strife is Neikos, divine beings who bind and loose the elements.[13]

Myths of initiation

The style in which the content of myth has been described here should not be equated with a 'symbolic' or 'allegorical' approach to myth. Nothing of that kind is intended. The images which form the content of the myth are not invented symbols for abstract truths. They are actual experiences in the soul of the initiates.

The initiates in the Mysteries experienced these images with spiritual organs of perception, as ordinary men experienced the impressions of their eyes and ears. Just as such impressions are nothing in themselves but must be evolved in perception through contact with an external object, so are the mythological images nothing unless they are activated by spiritual facts; the difference is only that in sense-perception a person is outside the objects, whereas the mythological images can only be a real experience when a person stands within the spiritual processes to which they correspond. And that means, as the ancient *mystai* knew, going through an initiation.[14]

The spiritual happenings which the initiate perceives are then given pictorial form by the images of the myth. It is impossible to understand the workings of myth unless we realize that it clothed in pictures actual spiritual experiences. The spiritual processes themselves are supersensible. The images, whose content is a reminiscence of the sense-perceptible world, are not themselves spiritual but only clothe the spiritual in pictures. To live merely in the images would be to dream. The spiritual experience is only accessible to those who are able to sense the reality behind the image, just as we sense the real rose through the impressions of our senses.

This is the reason too why mythological images are never unambiguous. Their character as pictorial illustrations means that the same myths may give expression to a variety of spiritual events. Hence it is not a contradiction when interpreters of myth relate a particular story now to one and now to another spiritual fact.

From this point of view we can follow a thread through the multiplicity of the Greek myths. To begin with we may consider the saga of Heracles. A new light is thrown upon the 'twelve labours' imposed on the hero, deepening their significance, when we notice that before the culminating, most difficult labour he has himself initiated in the Mysteries of Eleusis. In the service of Eurystheus, king of Mycenae, he has to descend into the underworld and bring back with him the hell-hound Cerberus. To enable him to descend into hell, Heracles has to be initiated: the role of the Mysteries was to lead a person through the death of the perishable nature, i.e. into the underworld. And through initiation, his eternal part was redeemed from the power of death. Thus it was that the *mystes* overcame death, and it is as an initiate that Heracles overcomes the dangers of the underworld.*

* The other 'labours' may therefore justifiably be interpreted as corresponding to stages in the soul's development. The conquest of the Nemean lion and his bringing it to Mycenae shows the hero mastering the purely physical power in human nature and taming it. Then his killing of the nine-headed Hydra, conquering it with firebrands and dipping his arrows in its gall, which made them unerring, shows him overcoming the lower, sense-derived knowledge by means of the fire of the spirit: by conquering it he gains the power of seeing lower things in the light of spiritual vision. Heracles captures the hind of Artemis, the divine huntress: he hunts down all that wild nature can offer to the soul

The voyage of the Argonauts can be similarly interpreted. Phrixus and his sister Helle, children of the Boeotian king, suffered badly at the hands of their stepmother. The gods sent them a ram with a golden fleece, which carried them away through the air. As they flew over the strait between Europe and Asia, Helle fell in and was drowned — which gives the strait its name: Hellespont. Phrixus however reached the king of Colchis on the eastern shore of the Black Sea, where he sacrificed the ram to the gods and gave its fleece to King Aeetes. He caused it to be hung up in a grove and guarded by a terrible dragon. It was the Greek hero Jason, in company with the other heroes Heracles, Theseus, Orpheus, etc., who undertook to fetch the fleece from Colchis.[15] Aeetes laid upon Jason severe conditions for the attainment of the fleece; but Medea, the king's daughter, was skilled in magic and came to his aid. He harnessed two fire-breathing bulls and ploughed a field, sowing it with dragon's teeth. When these sprang up into armed men, on Medea's advice he threw a stone amongst them, whereupon they turned and killed one another. It is by Medea's magic that Jason lulls the dragon to sleep and so wins the fleece. He then returns with it to Greece, taking Medea as his wife. The king pursues the fugitives, and in order to delay him Medea kills her little brother Apsyrtus and scatters his limbs in the sea. Aeetes pauses to collect then and so the pair reach Jason's homeland with the fleece.

Every detail of the story requires elucidation in depth. The fleece is something pertaining to man which is infinitely precious, something lost to him since the time of the beginning, and which can be recovered only by the overcoming of terrible powers — such is the situation with regard to the eternal in man's soul. The eternal belongs to man, yet he finds himself divided from it by his own lower nature, and he can only attain to it when he conquers and lulls to sleep

of man. The other labours may be similarly interpreted — the aim here was only to establish the general principle that they point to a process of inner development.

his lower self. That is made possible when the magic power of his own consciousness (Medea) comes to his aid. Medea becomes for Jason what Diotima was for Socrates when she instructed him in the Mysteries of love.[16] Man's own wisdom possesses the magic power of conquering the transitory and attaining to divinity. From his lower nature, on the other hand, only a debased humanity — the armed men — can spring: this is overcome by spiritual and intellectual means, the advice of Medea. But even when the hero has found the eternal — the fleece — he is not yet safe. A part of his consciousness — Apsyrtus — must be offered up as a sacrifice. This is demanded by the nature of the sense-perceptible world, which is only to be comprehended by us as a manifold, 'dismembered' domain.[17] We might go still further into the spiritual processes underlying these images, but the intention here is only to indicate the principle underlying the formation of myths.

Special interest attaches from this point of view to the saga of Prometheus. Prometheus and Epimetheus are sons of the Titan Iapetus. The Titans are the children of the oldest generation of the gods, Uranus (Heaven) and Gaia (Earth). Kronos, the youngest of the Titans, usurped his father's throne and seized the rulership of the world. He was overthrown in his turn by his son, Zeus, along with the other Titans; Zeus then became the supreme among the gods. In the titanomachy, Prometheus sided with Zeus and it was on his advice that Zeus banished the Titans to the underworld. Nevertheless the Titan disposition still lived on in Prometheus — he was only half a friend to Zeus. When Zeus was about to destroy mankind on account of their *hubris,* Prometheus took up their cause and taught them numbers, writing and that other prerequisite of culture, the use of fire.[18] This provoked Zeus' rage against Prometheus. Hephaestus, a son of Zeus, was commissioned to make a female form of great beauty, which all the gods adorned with every possible gift. She was named Pandora ('all-gifted'). The messenger of the gods, Hermes, brought her to Prometheus' brother, Epimetheus, to whom she gave a casket as a gift from the gods. Epimetheus accepted the gift despite the fact that Prometheus had warned him on no account to accept a gift from the gods. When the casket was opened, out flew every possible human affliction. Only Hope remained inside, because Pandora quickly shut the lid — and Hope exists still as a dubious free gift from heaven. As for Prometheus, on account of his relationship to man he was chained at Zeus' command to a crag in the Caucasus mountains. An eagle perpetually gnaws his liver, which as often grows again. He is to pass his days in agonizing loneliness, until one of the gods freely sacrifices himself, i.e. dedicates himself to death. Prometheus meanwhile bears his suffering with unflinching patience, for he knows that Zeus will be dethroned by the son of a mortal woman unless he himself becomes her husband. It was important for Zeus to know this mystery; he sent the messenger-god Hermes to Prometheus to enquire about it, but Prometheus refused to say anything. At this point the sagas of Heracles and of Prometheus are connected: in the course of his wanderings, Heracles reaches the Caucasus. He slays the eagle which gnawed at Prometheus' liver. And the centaur Chiron, who cannot die though he suffers from an incurable wound, sacrifices himself for Prometheus. The Titan is thereupon reconciled with the gods.

The Titans here are the force of the will — a force of nature (Kronos) originating from the primal spirit of things (Uranus). They are not an abstraction personified as 'forces of will,' but actual beings of will. Prometheus is one of them, which indicates his nature, but he is not wholly Titan: he belongs in some ways on the side of Zeus, i.e. the spiritual power which assumed cosmic rule when the unbridled force of nature — Kronos — had been quelled.

Prometheus is a representative of those worlds from which man draws his forward-striving will — which is half a nature-force and half a spiritual force. The will inclines to both good and evil. Indeed its destiny is fixed by its tendency either to the spiritual or the perishable; and this destiny is the destiny of man himself: chained to the perishable, gnawed by the eagle, he has to suffer. His ultimate goal can be reached only when he withdraws into solitude to seek his destiny. But he has a secret. It consists in this: the divine power — Zeus — must be married to a mortal, i.e. a consciousness bound to a physical human body, so as to beget a son — human wisdom — who will set free the god.

In this way consciousness achieves immortality. But the secret must not be betrayed until the coming of a *mystes* — Heracles — who overcomes the power that threatens him constantly with death. The centaur, a creature that is half animal, half man, has to sacrifice itself to redeem him: this is man himself, the man who is half animal and half spirit, who must die in order that the purely spiritual man may be released.

The gifts spurned by Prometheus, the human will, are taken up by Epimetheus — cleverness or shrewdness. But he gains nothing from them except troubles and sorrows. The rational mind clings to the inessential and perishable. Only one thing remains behind: the hope that even from the perishable the eternal may one day be born.[19]

The myth and Mysteries of Eleusis

The spirit of mysteriosophy is all-pervasive in the festivals celebrated at Eleusis in Greece in honour of Demeter and Dionysus. A 'sacred way' stretched to Eleusis from Athens, lined with mysterious signs intended to bring the soul into an exalted mood. At Eleusis itself there were mysterious temple-complexes,* under the direction of a priestly dynasty. The wisdom which qualified them for this task was handed from

* There is an instructive account of the layout of the sanctuaries in K. Bötticher, 'Ergänzungen zu den letzten Untersuchungen auf der Akropolis in Athen,' in *Philologus,* supplementary volume III, part 3. (See further: Mylonas, G., *Eleusis and the Eleusinian Mysteries,* Princeton 1961, especially Chapters VI and VII.)

generation to generation in the priestly families; it was the wisdom which enabled then to perform their ritual service at Eleusis, the wisdom of the Greek Mysteries, mysteriosophy.[20]

The festivals were celebrated twice in the course of each year, and dramatized the cosmic events governing the fate of the divine in the world and of the human soul. The Lesser Mysteries took place in February, the Greater Mysteries in September. Initiation into the Mysteries took place in connection with these festivals. The climax of the initiatory proceedings was a symbolic enactment of the human and cosmic drama on the site.

The temples at Eleusis were dedicated to the goddess Demeter.[21] She is a daughter of Kronos and, before his marriage to Hera, Zeus had by her a daughter, Persephone. Once, while Persephone was out playing, Pluto, the god of the underworld, carried her off. Demeter went wandering through the world lamenting and seeking for her. At Eleusis she sat down on a stone, and there she was found by the daughters of Celeus, a governor of Eleusis. In the form of an old woman she was taken into the service of the family of Celeus, as nurse to the queen's son. She wished to endow the son with immortality, and to this end she hid him every night in the fire.[22] But when his mother learned of it she cried and wailed, after which the bestowal of immortality was no longer possible and Demeter left the house. It was then that Celeus built the temple. The grief of Demeter for Persephone was boundless, and spread sterility over the earth. To avert total disaster, the gods had to find a way of appeasing her. So Zeus induced Pluto to let Persephone return to the upper world. However, before he let her go he gave her a pomegranate to eat and because of this she was compelled to return ever afterwards at regular intervals: for a third part of the year she dwelt in the underworld, and for two thirds in the upper world. Comforted, Demeter returned to Olympus. But she founded at Eleusis, where she had undergone her grief, the cult-festivals in which her fate was ever afterwards commemorated.

The mythology of Demeter and Persephone is not hard to interpret. It is the soul which lives alternately in the underworld and in the upper regions: the myth clothes in a picture the eternal nature of the soul which persists throughout its endless transformations, its births and deaths. The soul has an immortal mother — Demeter — but is carried away into the realms of transitoriness, and even induced to share in the destiny of the perishable world. It has eaten the fruit of the underworld, that is to say, the human soul has found satisfaction in perishable things, and therefore cannot live always in the heights where the gods abide. It has to return ever and again to the kingdom of transience.

Demeter stands for the essential source out of which human consciousness arises. Thus we must conceive of consciousness as arising from the spiritual forces of the Earth.[23] And the fact that through her the Earth is endowed with the regenerative power of the crops points to still deeper aspects of her nature. It is she who wishes to grant immortality to man — Demeter places her charge secretly in the fire every night. Man, however, cannot bear the pure energy of fire (or spirit) and Demeter has to cease her attempt. All she can do is to institute the temple cult. Through this, so far as he is able, man can participate in the divine nature.

The festivals at Eleusis were an eloquent confession of the belief in the immortality of the human soul. The conviction was expressed in the imagery of the myth about Persephone. But alongside Demeter and Persephone at Eleusis, the god Dionysus was honoured.[24] If Demeter stood for the divine origin of the eternal within man, Dionysus was worshipped as the divine presence in the world which assumes an endless variety of forms. He is the god poured out into cosmic existence, torn apart in order to be reborn spiritually. He rightly takes his place beside Demeter in the festivals.*

---

* The spirit of the Eleusinian Mysteries is brilliantly captured by Edouard Schuré in his *Sanctuaires d'Orient*, Paris 1898.

The Odyssey

The thread which runs through the sagas of the Argonauts, Heracles and Prometheus can also be traced through Homer's Odyssey.[25] The use of such a method of interpretation may seem forced: but on closer consideration of all that has been said, even the strongest doubts must be dispelled.

In the first place, it is a surprise to hear it said of Odysseus that he made a descent into the underworld [nekyia, Book XI]. Whatever theories we may hold about the author of the Odyssey, it is impossible to accept that he portrayed the descent of a mortal into the underworld without thereby relating him to the meaning of the descent in Greek thought — namely the conquest of transitoriness and the awakening of the eternal in the soul. Odysseus' feat must be presumed to achieve this, and his experiences thus take on a profounder significance, just as did those of Heracles: they become a description of something that does not belong to the world of sense-perception but rather to the inner development of the soul. That is why the narrative course of the Odyssey is not adapted to external events, but the hero voyages in enchanted ships, and geographical distances are handled in the most arbitrary fashion; the real and perceptible are not the point. It is easy to understand why, if the outward events are narrated in order to clothe in pictures a spiritual process. The poet himself says in the opening invocation that his poem treats of the search for the soul:

> Sing in me Muse! sing the tale of the man, the
>   resourceful hero,
> destroyer of Troy's holy towers, sing all that he suffered,
> the cities he saw, the men and ways that he learned there,
> buffeted long on the sea, enduring it all in his heart,
> seeking to save his own soul, and win his companions
>   their homeland.

This section originally in Chapter 5 of Christianity as Mystical Fact.

This is a man seeking for the soul — the divine in man — and it is his wandering on that quest that the poet will relate.

He comes to the land of the Cyclops, uncouth giants with one eye in their forehead. Polyphemus, the most horrifying of them, devours several of the travellers, but Odysseus saves himself by blinding the Cyclops. This refers to the first stage of life's pilgrimage: physical strength, the lower nature, has to broken, for if its power is not broken, if it is not blinded, it will devour you.

Then Odysseus reaches the island of the enchantress Circe, who transforms some of his companions into grunting swine, but he manages to subdue her. She is a spiritual power, but of a lower kind, still directed towards the transitory world. Spiritual power misused can have the effect of degrading man still deeper into animality. Odysseus has to master it. He is then able to descend into the underworld, becoming a *mystes*. The dangers to which he is subsequently exposed are those which beset the initiate in his progress from the lower to the higher stages: he passes the Sirens, who lure travellers to their death by means of the magic sweetness of their song — they are images of the lower imagination, the first objects of pursuit to those who have freed themselves from the limits of the senses. Odysseus grasps the spirit in its free creative activity but he is not yet an initiate: he is still chasing illusions, from whose power he must break loose. Odysseus has to accomplish the passage between Scylla and Charybdis — the novice vacillates between spirit and sense, not yet able to realize the full value of the spiritual, though the sense-world has lost its former meaning. A shipwreck ends the lives of all Odysseus' companions; he alone escapes, being befriended by the nymph Calypso who cares for him for seven years. Eventually, at the behest of Zeus, she permits him to return to his homeland. Here the *mystes* attains to a level where all his fellow aspirants fall short and only one, Odysseus, is found worthy. The one who is worthy enjoys for a time — seven years, in accordance with the number-symbolism of the Mysteries — the tranquillity of a gradual initiation-process.

But before reaching home, however, Odysseus is brought to the island of Phaeacia, where he is an honoured guest. The king's daughter takes his part, King Alcinous himself entertains and fetes him. Odysseus re-enters the world, meeting once again its delights — and the spirit of attachment to the world once more awakes in him! But he finds the way home, the way to the divine. His wife Penelope is besieged by a crowd of suitors, and has promised them that she will choose a husband when she has completed a garment that she is weaving. She evades keeping her promise by unravelling every night what she had woven during the day. Before he can rest, united again with his wife, Odysseus therefore has to overcome the suitors. The goddess Athene changes him into a beggar, so that he can enter unrecognized, and in this way the suitors are conquered.

What Odysseus is seeking is his own deeper consciousness, the divine powers in the soul. It is with these that he wishes to be united. But before the *mystes* can discover them, he has to conquer everything that comes as a suitor for the favour of his consciousness — that is, the world of mundane reality, transient nature, from which the horde of suitors stems. The logic that pertains to them is a weaving that unravels itself when it has been spun. Wisdom — the goddess Athene — is a sure guide to the deepest powers which the soul possesses. She turns a man into a beggar, meaning that she divests him of all that is transitory in origin.

3. From Myth to Philosophy: the pre-Socratics

Many histories of thought still proceed as though early humanity one day stopped believing in fairy-tales and myths, and began looking at what lay before their eyes and tried to understand it. Only quite recently have many historians begun to challenge this usually unstated assumption, which essentially veils a desire to confirm our own way of looking at things rather than to confront a different way of seeing: we look back, and conclude that early thinkers saw some things 'correctly' (i.e. as we do today) but in other ways were strangely confused and superstitious (i.e. different from us). One of Steiner's most brilliant contributions to thought is his realization that ways of understanding the world in earlier times were genuinely other than ours, and that indeed our own way of thinking evolved slowly out of older ones. There was never a point at which people just began to see what was really there — consciousness, including our own, always interprets, always sees from a certain perspective. He enables us to appreciate the coherence and truth of other perspectives, subtly feeling his way inside them. Ideas which we often suppose to have needed the shift to 'realistic' thought themselves turn out to derive from older, less familiar modes of consciousness. Steiner examines Heraclitus, for whom all things were temporary forms of a dynamic heat-energy, and Pythagoras, who originated the idea of mathematically and rationally investigable nature. In them, as in the transitional figure Pherecydes of Syros, rational thought is still involved in mythic imagery and a visionary experience of reality close to that conveyed in the Mysteries —

From: *Das Christentum als mystische Tatsache.* Complete translation of the section *'Die griechischen Weisen vor Plato im Lichte der Mysterienweisheit.'*

as the recently discovered Derveni papyrus, together with the Orphic gold plates and other objects also show. In Pherecydes we just start to see what had been felt as a deeper dimension within the myth becoming a structure of ideas that can be set over against the sense-content of the pictures. Far from being made obsolete by reason, the Mystery-process helps us to understand the emergence of reason itself.

Heraclitus of Ephesus

A whole range of considerations leads us to the conclusion that the ideas of the Greek philosophers depended upon the same way of thinking as the knowledge of the mystai.[1] The great philosophers only become comprehensible when we approach them with feelings gained in the study of the Mysteries. With what veneration does Plato speak of the 'secret teachings' in the Phaedo:

> Perhaps these people who direct the religious ini-
> tiations are close to the mark, and all the time there
> has been an allegorical meaning beneath their doctrine
> that he who enters the next world uninitiated and
> unenlightened shall lie in the mire, but he who
> arrives there purified and enlightened shall dwell
> among the gods. You know how the initiation
> practitioners say:
>   There are many who bear the sacred wands, but the
> Bacchoi are few.
>   Well, in my opinion these latter are simply those
> who have lived the philosophic life in the right way; I
> myself have done my best in every way to join that
> company, leaving nothing undone which I could do to
> attain this end.[2]

One who speaks about initiation in this way must indeed

have dedicated his search for wisdom to the way of thinking which was begotten by the Mysteries. And there is no doubt that a brilliant light is shed on the words of eminent Greek philosophers when that illumination comes from the Mysteries.

The relationship of Heraclitus of Ephesus (c.535–475 BC) to the Mysteries is immediately clear from a saying which is handed down about him, to the effect that his thoughts were 'an impassable road.' Anyone who was not an initiate would find in them nothing but 'obscurity and darkness,' but they were 'brighter than the sun' to those who approached them in the company of the *mystai*. It is said that his book was deposited by him in the temple of Artemis — indicating that he could only be understood by the initiated.[3] Heraclitus was called 'the Obscure,' because the key of the Mysteries alone cast light on his views.

In Heraclitus we witness a figure of the utmost earnestness in his approach to life. It is evident, when we reconstruct his thought in its essentials, that for him knowledge bore an inner meaning which words could gesture towards rather than directly express. It was out of some such realization that there arose his celebrated utterance: 'Everything is in flux.' Plutarch explains its meaning as follows:

> Heraclitus holds it impossible to go into the same river twice; no more can you grasp mortal being twice so as to hold it. So sharp and swift is change; it scatters and brings together again, not again, no nor afterwards; even while it is being formed it fails, it approaches, and it is gone.[4]

Heraclitus' thought sees through the nature of transitory things, and he is constrained to lay bare the essence of transitoriness in the sharpest terms conceivable. Such a characterization can only have come about because he was contrasting the transitory with the eternal.[5]

Nor could the characterization have been extended to

include man unless Heraclitus had seen into his inner nature. Yet he does include man under this characterization:

> Life and death — waking and sleeping — youth and age: are the same. This changes into that, and that into this.[6]

The saying connotes full cognition of the illusory nature of the lower personality. Still more radical is his saying:

> Both life and death are to be found in our living, and in our dying.[7]

What does this signify if not that a preference for life over death shows that we are only judging from the standpoint of the transitory? Death is a passing away — in order to make way for new life. The eternal lives in the new life, however, just as it did in the old. Whether in the passing life or in death it is the same eternal reality. The knowledge of this enables a man to face death or life with the same emotion. It is only when he has not been able to awaken the eternal within him that he attributes to life any special significance.

The saying 'All is in flux' can be repeated a thousand times, but it is vacuous unless it evokes this content of feeling. The acknowledgment of eternal becoming is worthless if it does not lift us above our attachment to transitoriness. Heraclitus indicates a renunciation of the sensual urge towards transitory enjoyments when he says:

> How can we claim that in ordinary life 'we are'? We know that from the vantage point of the eternal 'we are yet we are not.'

Or according to another fragment:

> Hades and Dionysus are one.[8]

Dionysus — god of the joy of life, of sprouting and growing, celebrated in the Dionysiac festivals — is for Heraclitus the same as Hades, god of death and destruction. The right perspective on the deficiencies and excellences of existence is granted only to those who see death in life and life in death, and in both the eternal that transcends both life and death. The deficiencies then become justified, since in them too the eternal is present. What they are from the standpoint of the limited, lower life turns out to be mere illusion:

> What people want is not always what is best for them.
> It is illness which makes health sweet and good;
> hunger that makes food satisfying; toil brings rest.[9]

> The sea is the purest and impurest water. For fish it is drinkable and salutary, but for men it is undrinkable and harmful.[10]

The primary thrust of Heraclitus' thought here is not the perishability of earthly things, but rather the splendour and sublimity of the eternal.

Heraclitus denounces Homer, Hesiod and the learned men of his time. His aim was to demonstrate the dependence of their thought on transitory things. He wanted nothing to do with gods whose qualities derived from the perishable world; nor could he exalt a form of knowledge that sought for laws in the flux of becoming and passing away. For him, there is something eternal which announces itself from the midst of the perishable.

For this eternal he has a profound metaphor:

> The connectedness of things is a tension between
> opposites, just as in a bow or a lyre.[11]

How much lies concealed in this metaphor! Tension in one direction is exactly balanced by that in the other, resulting in a unity and harmonization of forces. There are high and low notes; yet their contradictions are resolved in the musical scale. Heraclitus' thought extends the analogy to the spiritual world:

> Immortals are mortal, mortals immortal, living the
> other ones' death, dying the other ones' life.[2]

The primal fault for man was to fix his thought on change-able things, and so estrange himself from the eternal. Life became a danger to him. For all that happens to him comes from his life. The sting of this danger is removed, however, if he ceases to set an uncritical value on life. He regains his innocence. It is as though he abandons his serious attitude to life and regains his childhood. The child plays with many of the things taken so seriously by the adult. The Heraclitean thinker is like the child. 'Serious' issues lose their value when viewed from the eternal standpoint; life seems like play. 'Eternity,' says Heraclitus,

> is a child at play. It is the reign of a child.[13]

The beginning of error lies in taking too seriously a great deal that does not deserve it.

God has poured himself out into the world of things. To treat things apart from God is seriously to make them 'tombs of the divine.' To disport ourselves with them like a child is to turn our serious intent to rediscovering the underlying divinity, the God who sleeps spellbound in things.

There is a 'burning' process — a consuming fire — in the vision of the eternal when it acts upon our customary notions about the world. The spirit dissolves thoughts that derive from the senses, evaporates them, as a destructive fire. It is in this higher sense that Heraclitus considers fire to be the first principle of all things. Of course, it is primarily a straightforward explanation of physical phenomena. But is easy to misunderstand Heraclitus if we debate his concept of fire, asking whether he meant by it sense-perceptible fire or whether it was not rather a metaphor for the eternal spirit which dissolves and reconstitutes all things. For that is to misconstrue his thought. He meant both, yet neither of these things.* For him, the spirit was vitally active in ordinary fire. And the energy of physical fire works in a higher mode in the human soul, and in its crucible melts sense-perceptions down to draw forth from them the vision of the eternal.[14]

It is all too easy to misunderstand Heraclitus, for example when he makes war the father of things — but only of things, not of the eternal. If there were no contradictions in the world, if there were not the most diverse conflicting tendencies, there would indeed be no becoming, no transitory things. Yet diffused through this contradictoriness and revealing itself there is not war, but connectedness. For though there is war in all things, for that very reason the mind of the wise man should flame up over things and bring them into connectedness.

Here we come upon one of Heraclitus' great insights. For it is from such a viewpoint that he develops his answer to the question of man's individual identity. For man is com-posed of the warring elements, into which the Divinity is poured out. In that divided state he finds himself. In addi-tion, he becomes aware of the spirit, the *Logos*, which stems from the eternal. For him, however, the spirit comes to birth out of the clash of the elements. Indeed it is the spirit which brings the elements into equilibrium. Thus in man Nature transcends herself: all things are one, and it is the same power that made conflict and opposition which now in its wisdom reconciles them once again. Man lives in an eternal duality, in the contradiction between the flux of time and

---

* Philo of Alexandria, living around the beginning of the Christian era, still thinks in the same way. Considering the legal sections of the Bible he writes: 'There are those who take a purely symbolic view of the written Law. They inquire diligently after its spiritual meaning, but scorn the actual laws. But I can only blame such people, for they ought to observe both the hidden meaning and the obvious one.' Philo, *De migratione Abrahami*, 89.

eternity. Through the eternal *Logos* he attains to individual
existence, and must thenceforward fashion his higher being.
He lives in a state of dependence, but also independence. He
beholds the *Logos,* but he can only participate in it according
to the proportion of the mixture which the eternal *Logos*
brought about in his case. Hence derives his unique calling
— to fashion the eternal out of the temporal.

It is the spirit, the *Logos,* which works in him. But it does
so in a special way: out of the temporal. The uniqueness of
the human soul consists in this, that a temporal being is
active and powerful in the same way as an eternal being, and
can be likened both to a god and to a worm. Man has his
place between god and animal. The active, powerful compo-
nent of his being is his 'daimonic' part. It is that in him
which reaches out beyond his own self. As Heraclitus
strikingly puts it:

A man's *daimon** is his destiny.[15]

Thus for Heraclitus something far more extensive than
personality is to be found in man; personality is the vehicle
of the 'daimonic' self, which is not limited by the bounds of
his individual existence and for which personal dying and
being-born have no significance.

What has the 'daimonic' self to do with the transient form
of the personality? The personality is no more than a mode
of appearance for the *daimon.* The man who attains this
insight is able to look forwards and backward, beyond his
own self. The presence within him of the *daimon* is a sign to
him of his own eternal self, and this he can no longer limit
to the role of informing his particular personality; the
personality as such is simply one mode of appearance for the
daimon which cannot in principle be confined to a single
personal manifestation. It has the power to inhabit many
personalities, and may shift from personality to personality.

* *'Daimon'* is here used in its Greek sense of 'spiritual being.'

The important idea of reincarnation arises self-evidently from the premises of Heraclitus' thought. Or rather, not just the idea but the experience of reincarnation. The idea merely goes before the experience: for when a person becomes aware of the 'daimonic' self within him he does not find something guiltless and simple. The *daimon* possesses particular characteristics. Where do they originate? Why do I possess such predispositions?

It is because my *daimon* has been shaped by other personalities. And unless I am to assume that the task I have to accomplish in the *daimon* is fulfilled with my own personality, I am preparing another, future personality. Thus there is something which intervenes between myself and the cosmic 'One-and-All,' something which reaches out beyond myself but which is not yet the Godhead as such: it is my *daimon* which occupies this intermediary position. Today is simply the outcome of yesterday, and likewise this life is the outcome of a previous one — and the foundation for the next. Earthly man looks back over numerous yesterdays and forward to many tomorrows, and the wise soul upon many former lives and lives to come. The ideas and abilities I developed in the past, I make use of now — and does not life show us that people rise over the horizon of existence already with the most varied capacities? Surely this diversity of gifts does not come from nowhere.

Natural science currently congratulates itself on expelling from the domain of biology any notion of the miraculous. David Friedrich Strauss mentions it as one of the great achievements of the modern age that a whole living being is no longer regarded as springing into being out of nothing by an act of creation. Its wholeness and completeness is understood as a result of evolution from more primitive forms. The developed form of an ape no longer seems miraculous when we realize that it has arisen through the gradual modification of ancestral forms, going back originally to primaeval fishes. Is it not reasonable to assume the same conditions of evolution for the spirit as we know to prevail in nature? Does a

higher developed spirit emerge from the same conditions as
a primitive one — say, Goethe and a Hottentot? It is no more
possible for a fish to develop from the ancestors of an ape
than for Goethe's spirit to issue from the same spiritual
conditions as a savage; its spiritual ancestry is simply quite
different. Spirit as well as body are in a process of evolving.
Goethe's spirit has more stages of development behind it
than that of the savage. If we understand the idea of reincarnation in this evolutionary sense it need no longer be
pronounced unscientific.[16]

It is a matter of knowing how to interpret the content of
the soul — and of not leaping to the idea of the miraculous.
I am able to write, owing to the circumstance that I learned
how to do so; no-one is able to sit down, having never held
a pen, and write. What then of the man with the spark of
'genius'? — in some cases his talent seems to border on the
miraculous. Even here, the spark of 'genius' is something that
has emerged, that has been learned. When it shows itself in
a personality, we may call it something 'spiritual,' with the
proviso that we understand that this 'spiritual' was also
originally something learned, something acquired through
former lives before it appears as a spontaneous ability in a
later one.

It was in this form alone that the concept of everlasting life
hovered before the inner eye of Heraclitus and the early
Greek philosophers: they never spoke of the survival of the
empirical personality. Take, for example, the poem of
Empedocles where he speaks of those who appeal to a
'miraculous' creation:

> Childish and ignorant they — they do not reach far
>   with their thinking
> Who suppose that what has not existed can ever come
>   into being.
> Or that something may die away and wholly vanish
>   for ever![17]

> It never can happen that being should arise from what
>   never existed,
> Impossible also that being should ever fade into
>   nothing.
> For wherever being is shifted, it still will continue to
>   be.[18]

> Never will any believe who is wise and interprets his
>   thinking
> That only as long as they live what is called by the
>   name here of living
> Do men continue existing, receiving their joys and
>   their sorrows,
> Or that before they were born or when they are dead
>   they are nothing.[19]

In the case of Empedocles, no question concerning the existence of an eternal part in man is raised, but only the question concerning its nature and how it can be cherished and cultivated. It is assumed from the outset that man occupies a mediating position between the earthly and the divine.

His thought knows nothing of a God outside and transcending the world. The divine lives in human beings — though in a human way. It is the force in them which makes them strive to become more and more divine. Thinking in this way, one can say with Empedocles:

> When, set free from the body, released you rise to the
>   aether,
> You become divine, an immortal, escaped from the
>   power of death.[20]

Looking at human life from this perspective, the prospect of initiation into the magic circle of the Eternal becomes a real possibility. Forces which would not unfold under purely natural conditions of life must certainly be present in man,

and if they remain untapped his life will pass away unfructi-
fied. It was the role of the Mysteries, as it was the task set for
themselves by the Greek philosophers, to release those forces
and thereby to make man akin to the divine.

Thus we can understand Plato's assertion that he who
enters the next world uninitiated and unenlightened shall lie
in the mire, but he who arrives there purified and enlightened shall dwell among the gods. There is a concept of
immortality here whose meaning lies within the cosmic
order: everything whereby man strives to rouse the Eternal
to life within himself is done to increase the existential value
of the world — and emphatically not to turn man into an
inessential onlooker at things who merely images in his
cognitive life an objective order that is wholly independent
of the mind.[21] His power of knowledge is a higher creative
force in nature. What flashes like spiritual lightning within
him is a divinity, hitherto subdued by magic spells: without
his act of cognition, the god would lie fallow and have to
await another deliverer. Hence human personality has a
living meaning not just for itself and in itself, but for the
world. From the Mystery point of view, life far transcends
the limits of individual existence, making intelligible that
glimpse of the Eternal conveyed by the verses of Pindar:

> Blessed is he who has seen these things, and then
> is laid in the hollow earth. He knows life's end,
> he knows the beginning ordained by Zeus.[22]

We understand too those characteristic proud gestures of the
philosophers such as Heraclitus, who could justly say that
much had been revealed to them, since they attributed their
knowledge not to the transitory self but to the immortal
daimon within them.

It was a pride necessarily impressed also with the seal of
humility and modesty. That is shown by the words: all
knowledge of transitory things is as changeable as those
things themselves. For Heraclitus, Eternity is a game. It could

be called the most serious matter, were it not that the word 'serious' has been worn out by its application to mundane experiences. 'Eternal play' gives man a freedom from anxieties in life which he could not have if he took transitory conditions 'seriously.'

Pythagoras of Samos

I

On the ground of the Mysteries there also came into being an understanding of the world that was nevertheless different from that of Heraclitus. It sprang up in the communities founded in southern Italy by Pythagoras (sixth century BC). The Pythagoreans regarded numbers and geometrical forms, understood mathematically, as the foundation of reality. Aristotle says of them:

> The so-called Pythagoreans led the field in mathematics and their studies convinced them that the principles of that science were of universal application. Numbers, of course, are by their very nature (i.e. as the simplest of mathematical objects) the first of those principles; and the Pythagoreans thought they saw in numbers, rather than in fire or earth or water, many resemblances to things which exist or which come into being. Thus they identified with certain properties of number justice, soul or mind, opportunity, and indeed more or less everything. They also realized that the properties and ratios of musical scales depend on numbers. In a word, they saw that other things, in respect of the whole of their natures, resemble numbers, and that numbers are the primary elements of the whole of nature.[23]

From: *Das Christentum als mystische Tatsache.*

The study of natural phenomena by means of the mathematical sciences must always lead to a kind of Pythagoreanism.

If a string, of a specific length, is struck it generates a
particular note (pitch). Shorten the string in accordance with
certain numerical ratios, and other notes will be produced.
Thus pitch can be expressed in terms of numerical proportions. Physics likewise expresses relationships of colour in
numerical terms. And when two substances combine in a
compound, it happens always in certain specific quantities
which can be numerically expressed that the two substances
come together. The Pythagoreans paid special attention to
such instances of measure and proportions in nature.
Geometrical figures play a similar role in nature, for instance
in astronomy — the application of mathematics to the
heavenly bodies.

Central to the way of thinking developed by the Pythagoreans is the fact that man discovers numerical and geometrical laws purely through his own autonomous mental activity.
And when he turns his gaze to the natural world, things
obey the same laws which he has ascertained in his own
soul. If someone grasps the idea of an ellipse, he knows the
laws of the ellipse. The heavenly bodies are found to move
according to such laws which he has ascertained.* A direct
corollary of this is that the operations of the soul in man are
not an activity set apart from the rest of the world. What is
expressed in those operations is the pervasive cosmic order.
In the Pythagorean view, the senses reveal sense-perceptible
phenomena, but not the harmonious ordering principles
which regulate them. These harmonizing and ordering
principles must rather be discovered in the mind of man, if
he wishes to see them at work in outer nature. The deeper
meaning of the world, which is expressed as an eternal law
of necessity, makes its appearance in the human soul and

---

* Naturally I do not enter here into the astronomical views of the early
Pythagoreans. What is said about them here may be applied equally to
the ideas of modern Copernicanism.[23a]

first achieves immediacy and actuality there. The meaning of the cosmos is revealed in the soul.

That meaning is not to be found in what we perceive by sight, hearing or touch: it must be brought up from the hidden depths of the soul, for it is there that the eternal laws lie hidden. To find the eternal, one must go down into the psychic depths. In those depths is God — the eternal harmony of the cosmos.

Thus man's psyche is not limited to the confines of his body, enclosed in his skin; for what are born in the human soul are the laws which govern the stars in their courses. The soul is not confined by our personal consciousness. In fact the personality is no more than the instrument through which the cosmic order manifests itself. The spirit of Pythagoras is caught by one of the Church Fathers, Gregory of Nyssa, who declared:

> We are told that human nature is a paltry thing,
> confined and small — whereas God is infinitely great.
> How then can what is paltry embrace the infinite? Yet
> who says this? Was the infinite God shut up within
> the flesh as in a vessel? Even in our own life, our
> spiritual part is not shut in by the boundaries of the
> flesh. The physical substance of the body is subject to
> limitations in space, but the soul reaches out in
> thought to move freely through the whole creation.[24]

The soul does not coincide with the personality; its home is with infinity. From the Pythagorean point of view, it could only be foolishness to suppose that the power of the soul is exhausted in its personal expression. For the Pythagoreans as for Heraclitus, the point was the awakening within the personality of the Eternal.

Knowledge to them meant an encounter with the Eternal. They valued a person exactly in the degree to which he brought the Eternal to manifestation. Life in a Pythagorean community consisted in fostering that sense of an encounter with the Eternal, and their education was designed to bring the members to such an experience. Their education was thus a philosophical initiation — the Pythagoreans could well say that in their mode of life they were striving for a goal similar to that of the Mystery-cults.[25]

II

In this connection it is quite true to say of Pythagoras and his pupils that they worshipped different gods from those of the people. Hence arises that gulf which divides a spirit such as Pythagoras from the ordinary people who are happy with the gods they have, whereas he has to consider them as belonging to the sphere of the imperfect and incomplete. This is where we must look for the 'Mystery' frequently mentioned in the context of Pythagoras — the Mystery that was not to be betrayed to the uninitiated.[26] It is essentially this: his thought attributed to the human soul an origin quite distinct from that of the gods of public religion. It was ultimately because of this 'Mystery' that Pythagoras drew upon himself so much of the hostility he experienced. How was he to explain — except to those whom he carefully prepared to comprehend it — that their own souls could be regarded as superior to the public divinities? And how was it possible, except within the strictly organized life of a brotherhood, to bring them to an awareness at once of their souls' exalted origin and their implication in the imperfect world? Imperfection became the spur to organize life in such a way that it led back, through a process of self-perfecting, to those origins.

It is understandable that Pythagoras' aspirations necessarily attracted around themselves legendary and mythical accretions. In fact, little or nothing of historical value about his personality has come down to us. Nevertheless, the picture I have given makes recognizable sense when taken against

From *Die Rätsel der Philosophie* (original edition 1914; GA no. 18), Part I, Chapter 2.

the background of various stories and legends considered as a whole.

A disturbing feature (from the modern point of view) in the picture of Pythagoras as it has come down is the doctrine of the so-called 'transmigration of souls.'[27] It seems naive that Pythagoras should have thought that he had lived in earlier times as another person. Yet it is worth mentioning that the great representative of the Enlightenment, Lessing, put forward a new form of the teaching of reincarnation in his treatise, *The Education of the Human Race* (1780) — though he arrived at the idea quite independently of the Pythagorean way of thinking. The progress of humanity seemed intelligible to Lessing only if human souls participated many times in life during the successive periods of time on earth. A soul's special abilities, etc. are brought with it into a later life from its experience in earlier ages. To Lessing it seemed natural that the soul should often have inhabited an earthly body, and it would inhabit one often in the future, struggling through many lives towards its greatest possible perfection. The idea of repeated lives on earth, he pointed out, is not unworthy of belief simply because it existed in archaic times — times 'when the human mind had not yet been led astray and weakened by the sophistries of the scholastics.'

The idea of reincarnation is found in Pythagoras, as it is in Pherecydes, who is mentioned in antiquity as his teacher. But it would be erroneous to suppose that he arrived at it by accepting a logical argument to the effect that the human soul, on its journey back to its origins, would require more than one earthly life. We mistake Pythagoras if we attribute that kind of intellectual process to him. Rather are we told of his tremendous journeyings; and that he consulted together with the sages who preserved traditions of the most ancient human conceptions. Studying those ideas of archaic man, we soon realize that the concept of reincarnation was extremely widespread in prehistoric times. Pythagoras linked on to archaic doctrines.[28] He necessarily regarded the mythological teachings and symbols he found in his own culture as decayed remnants of what had once been higher ideas. In his own time, the pictorial teachings had to be transformed into a world-picture that was accessible to thought.

Yet the conceptual world-picture figured only as part of the life of the soul. If this part were deepened, it would lead the soul back to its origins. But when the soul deepened its inner life in this way it discovered, through actual self-perception, its repeated lives. It cannot reach its own origins except by finding its way through repeated earthly lives. Like a traveller to a far-off land, passing through various localities on the way, the soul on its journey to 'the Mothers' traverses its previous lives, and the route by which it descended from its pristine perfection to its present fallen state. All in all, due consideration of the evidence leaves no room for us to doubt that Pythagoras reached his idea of reincarnation through 'inner perception' in this sense, rather than through a process of logical definition.

Pherecydes of Syros

The transition from the ancient picture-experience to conceptual experience can be seen happening at different times among the several cultures of mankind. In Greece, we can eavesdrop on the process by turning our attention to a particular figure: Pherecydes of Syros.[29]

Pherecydes inhabited a world of ideas which participated equally in the picture-experience and in conceptual life. The soul can only bring before itself his three primary concepts — Zeus, Chronos and Chthon — in a way that gives it the sense of belonging to the events of the external world.[30] It lives the three pictures, and it would be a mistake to be misled into seeing them, as anything like the usual concepts of modern-day thought. Chronos cannot be equated with 'time' as we think of it today. In contemporary terms, we can

From *Die Rätsel der Philosophie* (original edition 1914; GA no. 18), Part I, Chapter 2.

certainly call his Chronos a 'conceptual' entity, so long as we do not suppose that its meaning is thereby exhausted. Chronos is alive; its activity consists in devouring and consuming another entity, Chthon. Chronos is a ruling power in nature, and a ruling power in man. And in both man and nature Chronos is consuming Chthon. There is no point in asking whether the consuming of Chthon by Chronos is an inner experience or one belonging to the events of outer nature. It happens equally to both.

Connected with these two entities is Zeus. It is quite inadequate to treat Pherecydes' concept of Zeus as merely that of what we would call a mythological being, a god. But neither is he simply 'space' as we conceive it, though he is the entity in which the interaction between Chronos and Chthon takes place, and takes on spatial extension.

The interplay between Chronos, Chthon and Zeus is for Pherecydes primarily a picture-experience. It comes to consciousness rather in the way that one is aware of eating; but at the same time it is felt to belong to the external world in the manner of the experience of blue or red. We can put it in the following way. Consider fire in the act of burning things up: in the fire's activity, in the heat, lies Chronos. It is by looking to the activity of the fire, and, instead of forming a concept, holding fast to the image-content, that we can see 'Chronos'; it is then that we see, along with the activity of the fire (rather than the fiery substance), what Pherecydes means by 'Time.' No other conception of time is possible before the birth of rational thought. What we call time today is a real idea only for the age of the rational understanding of the world.

Or consider water — not as the thing, water, but consider it as it changes into air or vapour; or consider the clouds as they dissolve away. That is the picture-experience of Zeus: the activity of spreading through space, of radiant expansion as one might say. Or if we take water as it solidifies, or a solid as it liquefies, we are seeing Chthon. As the rational view of the world emerged into a later stage, Chthon turned into the idea of substance or matter, Zeus into the aether or space, and Chronos into time.

The interaction of these three principles constitutes for Pherecydes the sum of total reality. From it arises on the one hand the perceptible substances of the cosmos, fire, air, water, earth, and on the other a series of invisible, imperceptible and spiritual entities, who live in the worlds of material substance. Zeus, Chronos and Chthon could be interpreted to mean spirit, soul and matter — though the correlation is only approximate. It is really only through the interconnection of the three primary beings that the more material realms (fire, air, water, earth) and the psychic or spiritual (supersensible) entities alike come into being. If we wish to use slightly later expressions, we may designate Zeus as space/aether, Chronos as time/creator and Chthon as matter/producer. They are the three 'Mothers' of the world — still mentioned by Goethe where, in the Second Part of *Faust,* his hero makes the descent 'to the Mothers.'

The appearance of these three Mother-principles in Pherecydes makes us think of ideas among his predecessors the Orphics, as they are called. Their understanding and representation of the world still belonged, however, entirely to the old pictorial mode.[31] In them we already find the three primordials; Zeus, Chronos and Chaos. Yet in comparison with the three 'Mothers' of Orphic sources, those of Pherecydes are markedly less pictorial. We attempted to grasp in terms of thought what the Orphics were content to possess purely in the form of an image. Hence his place in history at what may be termed the very birth of thinking. The more conceptual nature of Pherecydes' presentation of Orphic ideas manifests itself nowhere so much as in the dominant mood of his soul, striking a note that was to be echoed among his various successors in early Greek philosophy. He felt constrained to acknowledge 'the Good' as the source of all things — a notion which he found quite at variance with the old mythologies about the world of the gods. The soul-qualities that belonged to the mythological world did not quite square with his fundamental idea at all. But Pherecydes could take for the quality of his three 'first principles' nothing other than 'the Good,' perfection.[32]

Hence we see that the birth of thought led to the dissolution of man's whole former way of feeling and experiencing. This inner crisis should not be overlooked when considering the emergence of the conceptual world-view.

The beginnings of thought could not have been experienced as a step forward if there had not been present the conviction that thinking is able to grasp things more perfectly than the old picture-experience. Of course, the feeling I mean to indicate could not have been clearly articulated at that stage of development. But in retrospect it stands out clearly as something that was indeed felt by the early Greek thinkers: the sense that the inherited image-world of their predecessors did not enable them to reach the highest and most perfect principles of things. The pictures were only able to reveal derivative, secondary principles. Thinking had to rise towards the higher principles, of which the content of the images was merely the outer expression.

The advance to conceptual thinking polarized the world as it was conceived into a more natural and a more spiritual sphere. The spiritual sphere was felt to contain, for the first time in a purely spiritual form, the meaning of what had formerly been picture-experience. There arose the quite new idea of something transcending the older spiritual world and the world of nature alike. This was the sublime goal of thinking. And it was on this sublime level that Pherecydes sought for his three Mother-principles. A phenomenological approach will show the kind of ideas which gripped a personality such as Pherecydes. In his environment, man discovers a fundamental harmony which is manifested in the course of the stars, the succession of the seasons with the blessings of the growing plants, etc. But into this beneficent order of things irrupt harmful, disruptive forces in the form of devastation by the weather, earthquakes, and so forth. Such a view leads to a sense of the dualism of opposed ruling powers; at the same time, the human soul clings to its conviction of an underlying unity. It is natural to assume that the ravaging hail, and the earthquake's destructive might, must ultimately spring from the same source as the benefi- cent order of the seasons. Looking through the good and the bad, man discerns beyond them a primal Goodness, at work in the earthquake as in the blessings of spring, in the withering heat of the sun as in the ripening of the seed, so that even in harmful events it is the good 'Mothers' who are at work. In this way, a tremendous riddle of the universe comes before the soul. To solve it, Pherecydes turns to his Ophioneus. He is dependent for Ophioneus on the old pictorial consciousness, where he is a sort of 'world-serpent.' He is actually a spiritual being, who, like all other cosmic beings, is numbered among the children of Chronos, Zeus and Chthon. But after his generation he has turned against the good first principles in his activities. Thus the world now falls into three parts: the first principles, designated as good, as perfect; the beneficent processes of the world; the destruc- tive, or at least imperfect world-processes which, as Ophio- neus, are woven into the beneficent events of the world.

Pherecydes' Ophioneus is not merely a symbol, standing for the destructive or pernicious powers of the universe. Because he stands on the very border between image and concept, it is not a matter of Pherecydes thinking, 'There are destructive forces, and these I represent in the figure of Ophioneus'; it is not a matter of a thought-process which is then clothed in imagination. When he sees destructive forces at work, before his soul is Ophioneus in immediate actuality, perceived as directly as the redness in a rose.

The difference between events relating to the good first principles ('Mothers') and those relating to Ophioneus is not clearly grasped by the pictorial consciousness. The need for the distinction first arose on crossing the threshold into conceptual thought. For it is at that juncture that the soul comes to feel itself as estranged and alone. It feels the need to question its own origins — and to seek those origins in the depths of the universe where Chronos, Zeus and Chthon are not as yet confronted by their opposite. At the same time, the soul feels that its own origin remains for the present unfathomable. For its sphere of self-observation is limited to the world in which the good first principles interact with Ophioneus, so that perfect and imperfect are all mixed up together. Ophioneus is twisted into the soul's own nature.

It is by absorbing oneself in their characteristic way of seeing that one can feel what was happening in the souls of certain figures in the sixth century BC, and how it seemed to them that the older divine beings of mythology were still entangled in the realm of the imperfect — still belonged, in fact, to the same imperfect world as themselves.

4. Platonic Mysteries

Plato's thought has permeated almost all our modern attitudes in one way or another, whether focused on ourselves or the world. That being so, much about it remains hard to interpret, ambiguous and alien in expression to modern readers. The inconclusive dialogue form, in which several views are explored dialectically, the frequent resort to myth and parable, suggest that Plato did not simply want us to accept his ideas, or even to follow the logic of his deductions. Often it appears that he is steering us rather toward some kind of breakthrough-experience, some sudden illumination or realization. Steiner is especially valuable for the way he reminds us of the process of Plato's thought, and the alien dimension which we so often sense begins to take shape as a further connection to the world of the Mysteries. The 'divine' status of knowledge, the complex searching for an illuminative vision, the analogy with Orphic and Eleusinian myth made sense to Steiner long before scholars have tentatively begun to explore the issue today.

The Mystery of immortality

The significance of the Mysteries for the intellectual life of the ancient Greeks can be appreciated when we look at the case of Plato's idea of the world. There is in fact only one way of making Plato fully intelligible, and that is to place him in the light that streams from the Mysteries. According to his later followers, the Neoplatonists, he taught an esoteric

From: *Das Christentum als mystische Tatsache.* Complete translation of the section *'Plato als Mystiker.'*

doctrine to those he admitted as worthy to receive it, and placed them under a 'seal of secrecy.'[1] His teaching was regarded as secret in the same way as mysteriosophy was secret.

For our purposes it matters little whether or not the Seventh Letter attributed to Plato is genuine — it has been disputed:[2] he, or someone else, expressed in the Letter the essentials of Plato's attitude to the world. Take the following passage from the Letter:

> But this much at any rate I can affirm about any present or future writers who pretend to knowledge of the matters with which I concern myself, whether they claim to have been taught by me or by a third party or to have discovered the truth for themselves; in my judgment it is impossible that they should have any understanding of the subject. No treatise by me concerning it exists or ever will exist. It is not something that can be put into words like other branches of learning; only after long partnership in a common life devoted to this very thing does truth flash upon the soul like a flame kindled by a leaping spark, and once it is born there it nourishes itself thereafter.[3]

The words might be taken to signify merely the inadequacy of verbal expression, a personal failing on the part of the writer, if we did not detect in them a Mystery-sense. Something that cannot and never will be put into words by Plato, must refer to a matter about which all writing would be futile: it must mean a feeling, a sense or experience that cannot readily be communicated, but can be gained only by 'long partnership in a common life.' This indicates a special process of education given by Plato to the elect, who caught the fire that flashed from his words; whereas others received only ideas.

Interpreting Plato's Dialogues depends very much on the

manner of approach we adopt. Everyone, according to his or her spiritual condition, will find in them either more or less significance. What took place between Plato and his pupils was much more than the imparting of the words in their literal meaning. Studying with him meant living in the atmosphere of a Mystery: the words possessed overtones and resonances which could only be heard, however, in the atmosphere of the Mystery; outside it, they died away unheard.[4]

The personality who stands at the centre of the world we encounter in Plato's Dialogues is Socrates. We need not concern ourselves here with the actual, historical Socrates, but only the figure as he is presented by Plato. Through his death, as a martyr to truth, Socrates assumes a kind of saintliness. He died in the unique manner of an initiate, for whom death is simply another phase of life. He encountered death just as he would any other circumstance, and such was his bearing that even among his friends the usual feelings connected with death were not stirred up. In the dialogue on the immortality of the soul, Phaedo says:

> My own feelings at the time were quite extraordinary.
> It never occurred to me to feel sorry for him, as you
> might have expected me to feel at the deathbed of a
> very dear friend. The Master seemed quite happy,
> Echecrates, both in his manner and in what he said; he
> met his death so fearlessly and nobly. I could not help
> feeling that even on his way to the other world he
> would be under the providence of God, and that when
> he arrived there all would be well with him, if it ever
> has been so with anybody. So I felt no sorrow at all, as
> you might have expected on such a solemn occasion;
> and at the same time I felt no pleasure at being
> occupied in our usual philosophical discussions — that
> was the form our conversation took; I felt an absolutely
> incomprehensible emotion, a sort of curious blend of
> pleasure and pain combined, as my mind took it in
> that in a little while my friend was going to die.[5]

The dying Socrates discourses to his pupils on the theme of immortality. As one who has realized the worthlessness of life, he furnishes a kind of proof utterly distinct from any logical, rational arguments. It seems as if it were not a man speaking — the man who is passing away — but eternal truth itself which had taken up its abode in a transitory personality. The atmosphere where truth can resound seems to be found where the temporal reality dissolves into nothingness.

We hear nothing in the way of logical proofs of immortality. The entire discourse is designed to conduct his friends to a vision of the eternal. At that point they will require no proofs. What would be the point of proving that a rose is red to a man who can see it? What would be the point of proving the eternity of spirit to one whose eyes are open to the spirit?

Socrates directs our attention to concrete events, actual experiences — above all to the experience of wisdom, and the fundamental quality of the struggle for wisdom: the struggle to free oneself from the superficial impressions of the senses, and to find the spirit within the world of the senses. Is that not in fact something equivalent to a kind of death? So at any rate thinks Socrates:

> Those who really apply themselves in the right way to
> philosophy are directly and of their own accord
> preparing themselves for dying and death, even if
> ordinary people seem not to realize it. If this is true,
> and they have actually been looking forward to death
> all their lives, it would of course be absurd to be
> troubled when the thing comes for which they have so
> long been preparing and looking forward.[6]

And he reinforces this by asking one of his friends:

> Do you think that it is right for a philosopher to
> concern himself with the so-called pleasures connected

with food and drink? ... What about sexual plea-
sures? ... And what about the other attentions that we
pay to our bodies? Do you think that a philosopher
attaches any importance to them? I mean things like
providing himself with smart clothes and shoes and
other bodily ornaments; do you think that he values
them or despises them — in so far as there is no real
necessity for him to go in for that sort of thing? ... Is it
not your opinion in general that a man of this kind is
not concerned with the body, but keeps his attention
directed as much as he can away from it and towards
the soul? ... In this, then — in despising the body and
avoiding it, and endeavouring to become independent
— the philosopher's soul is ahead of all the rest.[7]

In conclusion, says Socrates, the pursuit of wisdom has this
much in common with dying, that it leads man away from
the body.

But to what does it lead him? To the spiritual. Socrates
takes up the theme:

Now take the acquisition of knowledge; is the body a
hindrance or not, if one takes it into partnership to
share an investigation? What I mean is this: is there
any certainty in human sight and hearing, or is it true,
as the poets are always dinning into our ears, that we
neither hear nor see anything accurately? ... Then
when is it that the soul attains to truth? When it tries
to investigate anything with the help of the body, it is
obviously led astray.[8]

Everything we perceive with the help of bodily organs is
subject to generation and decay: that is the very reason we
are deluded. It is only the deeper insight into things fur-
nished by reason that enables us to participate in their
timeless truth. Hence the senses do not show the eternal to
us in its Real form, and if we trust them uncritically they

become delusive. They cease to be so when we confront them with the evidences of rational insight, and put their results to the test of insight derived from thought.[9]

Now, how would it be possible for reason to pass judgment on the things of sense if there were not within it something which transcended sense-perception? If that is so, then, our faculty of distinguishing true things from false must be set in opposition to our bodily senses and is not subject to the conditions which bind them. In particular it cannot be subject to the law to coming-to-be and passing-away, for it contains in it the True, which has no yesterday or today, and unlike the things of sense cannot fluctuate from one day to another. The True must itself be eternal. And in so far as the philosopher turns away from the perishable objects of sense and turns towards the True, he enters the domain of the eternal which dwells within him. And if we immerse ourselves totally in the spirit, we are living totally in the True. The sense-world is simply no longer there for us in its merely sensible form. Socrates says:

> Don't you think that the person who is likely to
> succeed in this attempt most perfectly is the one who
> approaches each object, as far as possible, with the
> unaided intellect, without taking account of any sense
> of sight in his thinking, or dragging any other sense
> into his reckoning — the man who pursues truth by
> applying his pure and unadulterated thought to the
> pure and unadulterated object, cutting himself off as
> much as possible from his eyes and ears and virtually
> all the rest of his body, as an impediment which by its
> presence prevents the soul from attaining to truth and
> clear thinking?[10]

And a little later:

> Is not what we call death a freeing and separation of
> soul from body? ... And the desire to free the soul is

found chiefly, or rather only, in the true philosopher;
in fact the philosopher's occupation consists precisely
in the freeing and separation of soul from body. ...
Well then, as I said at the beginning, if a man has
trained himself throughout his life to live in a state as
close as possible to death, would it not be ridiculous
for him to be distressed when death comes to him? ...
Then it is a fact, Simmias, that true philosophers make
dying their profession, and that to them of all men
death is least alarming.[11]

All higher moral action springs also, for Socrates, from the
liberation of the soul from the body. Anyone who just
follows the promptings of the body is not behaving mor-
ally. Socrates asks: Who is that we call valiant? The man
who, rather than following the body, follows the dictates of
the spirit, even when these imperil the body. And who
shows self-control? Is it not called self-control when we see
someone

not being carried away by the desires, but preserving
a decent indifference towards them; is not this
appropriate only to those who regard the body with
the greatest indifference and spend their lives in
philosophy?[12]

And Socrates treats all the other virtues in like manner.
He then goes on to characterize intellectual insight itself.
What is it that we call 'knowing' as such? Without doubt,
knowing is attained by the forming of judgments: I form a
judgment about some object before me, e.g. that the thing in
front of me is a tree. Now, how do I reach that assertion?
Only by knowing already what a tree is, and recollecting my
idea of a tree. A tree is a perceptible thing; thus when I
recollect a tree, I am recalling at the same time a perceptible
object and in saying that something is a tree I am likening it
to other things which have formerly been objects of my

perception and which I know are trees. In this sense knowledge is dependent on the power of recollection.

Recollection permits me to compare with one another the multiplicity of perceptible things; but this does not explain the sum total of my knowledge. Suppose I see two things which are alike, and form the judgment: 'These things are alike.' But in actuality no two things are exactly alike, only alike in certain particular ways. The idea of likeness therefore cannot arise from perceived actuality, but is independent of it. It comes to my aid in forming a judgment — just as recollection helps towards judgment, towards knowledge when, in the case of a tree, I recall other trees. In the case of two things related in particular ways, I recollect the idea of likeness. Ideas thus come before me in the same way as recollections but without being dependent on perceived actuality. All kinds of knowledge which are not derived from sense-perception rely on such ideas. The field of mathematics consists entirely of such ideas. It would be a poor geometrician who could only deal mathematically with things he could see or touch! In this way we have thoughts which are not derived from transitory outer nature but arise purely spiritually. And it is these very ideas which show all the marks of timeless truth. The content of mathematics will be eternally valid — even if the universe were to go to pieces tomorrow and a completely new world arise. The conditions of a new world-order might be such as to render current mathematical ideas inapplicable; but they would remain intrinsically valid in themselves.

When the soul withdraws into itself, it is able to bring forth such eternal ideas: only then. Therefore the soul is akin to the True, the Eternal, not to the transitoriness and appearance of the sense-world.[13] Hence Socrates asserts:

> But when the soul investigates by itself, it passes into
> the realm of the pure and everlasting and immortal
> and changeless; and being of a kindred nature, when
> it is once independent and free from interference,

consorts with it always and strays no longer, but
remains, in that realm of the absolute, constant and
invariable, through contact with beings of the same
nature. And this condition of the soul we call Wisdom.
... Now, see whether this is our conclusion from all
that we have said. The soul is most like that which is
divine, immortal, intelligible, uniform, indissoluble,
and ever self-consistent and invariable, whereas body
is most like that which is human, mortal, multiform,
unintelligible, dissoluble, and never self-consistent. ...
Very well; if this is the soul's condition, then it departs
at death to that place which is, like itself, invisible,
divine, immortal and wise; where, on its arrival,
happiness awaits it, and release from uncertainty and
folly, from fears and uncontrolled desires, and all
other human evils; and where (as they say of the
initiates in the Mysteries) it really spends the rest of
time with God.[14]

It is not the aim here to summarize all the ways in which
Socrates leads his friends to the Eternal. For the spirit of all
of them is the same: all point to the difference between the
path of the changeable impressions of the senses and that of
the mind alone with itself. It is to the inherent character of
the spiritual that Socrates points his hearers. If they can find
this out, they will see for themselves with the inner eye that
it is eternal.

The dying Socrates does not give a proof of immortality.
He simply lays bare the nature of the soul. And then it
transpires that coming-to-be and passing-away, birth and
death, have nothing to do with the essential soul. This has its
being in the True; and the True cannot come into existence
nor pass away. The soul and becoming can have no more to
do with one another than an odd number with an even
number. But death belongs to the process of becoming.
Hence the soul can have nothing to do with death. How can
we do other than admit that the immortal can as little

participate in mortality as the even in the odd? And, continues Socrates:

> If what is immortal is also imperishable, it is
> impossible that at the approach of death soul should
> cease to be. It follows from what we have already
> said that it cannot admit death, or be dead; just as
> we said that three cannot be even, or any odd
> number.[15]

Surveying the whole course of the dialogue conducted by Socrates — which leads to a perception of the Eternal in human individual existence — his hearers take up his ideas; they search in themselves for something that will answer in the affirmative to those ideas from their own experience; they make objections as these occur to them. But what has happened by the end of the dialogue? They have discovered something within themselves which they did not formerly possess. They have not just acquired abstract knowledge, but have gone through a process, and something has stirred to life in them which was not previously there. Is that not comparable with an initiation?[16] Is that not the reason why Plato chooses to set forth his philosophy in dialogue form? — it is a literary Mystery, exactly analogous to the processes that took place at the centres of initiation.

There are many places in his writings where Plato testifies to this in his own words. Plato's aim as a teacher of philosophy was to be a hierophant, in so far as this was possible in the philosophical medium. Clearly Plato realized the agreement of his methods with those of the Mysteries, and regards them as successful precisely when they lead to the goals which the *mystai* too would reach. Thus he says in the *Timaeus*:

> Of course everyone with the least sense always calls
> on God at the beginning of any undertaking, small or
> great. So surely, if we are not quite crazy, as we

embark on our account of how the universe began, or perhaps had no beginning, we must pray to all the gods and goddesses that what we say will be pleasing to them first, and then to ourselves.[17]

Plato promises those who follow such a course that 'some protecting deity will see us safely through a strange and unusual argument and bring us to a likely conclusion.'[18]

The Mystery of creation

It is in the *Timaeus* above all that the Platonic world-view stands revealed in its character of a Mystery. From the very beginning of the dialogue the conversation concerns an 'initiation': Solon is 'initiated' into the Mysteries of creation and into the mythological traditions which use pictures to symbolize eternal truth by an Egyptian priest. 'There have been and will be many different calamities to destroy mankind,' the priest tells Solon:

> The greatest of them by fire and water, lesser ones by countless other means. Your own story of how Phaethon, child of the sun, harnessed his father's chariot, but was unable to guide it along his father's course and so burnt up things on the earth and was himself destroyed by a thunderbolt, is a mythical version of the truth that there is at long intervals a variation in the course of the heavenly bodies and a consequent widespread destruction by fire of things on the earth.[19]

This passage in the *Timaeus* demonstrates the attitude of the initiates to the well-known myths. They see through to the truth that is veiled behind their imagery.

As the cosmogonic drama unfolds in the *Timaeus*, we are led by following the traces that point back to the origin of the

world to an intimation of the primordial power, out of which
everything came into existence:

> For to discover the maker and Father of this universe
> is indeed a hard task — and having found him it
> would be impossible to tell everyone about him.[20]

The *mystai* understand the force of that world 'impossible.'
It points towards the inner drama of the Godhead. For them,
God is not revealed in the materially comprehensible world,
where he is manifest only as nature, in which he lies under
a spell. He can be apprehended, as was taught in the Mysteries, only by one who awakens the divine in himself. That
is why he cannot be made intelligible to everyone.

But even to one who draws near to him, he does not
appear in his own nature. This too is explained in the
Timaeus.

The Father made the universe out of the world-body and
world-soul. He mixed the elements, in harmony and perfect
proportion — elements which he himself brought into being
by pouring himself out, giving up his separate existence.
Thus he produced the world-body. And stretched out upon
it, in the form of a cross, is the world-soul, the divine
presence in the world. It suffers death on this cross so that
the world can exist. And Plato therefore calls nature the
'tomb' of the divine — not however a tomb in which lies
something dead, but the tomb where lies the Eternal, for
which death is nothing but the opportunity to demonstrate
the omnipotence of life! Hence the right way to look upon
nature is for man to undertake the rescue of the crucified
world-soul, which should rise, released from death, released
from the spell which binds it. And where can this happen
except in the soul of an initiated man? Thus wisdom takes on
its proper meaning in a cosmic setting: knowledge is the
resurrection, the liberation of God.

In the *Timaeus* the world is presented developing out of the
imperfect into the perfect. The concept is one of progressive

process, of beings developing; and in this process God reveals himself. Coming-into-being is the resurrection of God from the 'tomb.' And within this development man makes his appearance. Plato demonstrates that with him something unique enters in. Now of course for Plato the whole world is itself a divine being, and man is not more divine than other beings. But in other beings God is present only in a hidden manner, in man he is manifest. The *Timaeus* concludes with the words:

> We can now claim that our account of the universe is complete. For our world has now received its full complement of living creatures, mortal and immortal; it is a visible living creature, it contains all creatures that are visible and is itself an image of the intelligible; and it has thus become a visible god, supreme in greatness and excellence, beauty and perfection, a single, uniquely created heaven.[21]

But this single and uniquely created world would not be perfect if it did not contain among its images the image of its Creator himself. And that image can arise only from the soul of man: it is not the Father himself, but the Son, the living child of God in the soul who is of like nature with the Father, to whom man can give birth.

The expression 'Son of God' is used in this context by Philo of Alexandria, who was called a Plato *redivivus*. It designates the Wisdom which lives in the soul and is born of man, having as its content the reason immanent in the world; while this world-reason — *Logos* – figures as the book in which 'every permanent characteristic of the world is recorded and inscribed.'[22] Or elsewhere it is the 'Son of God':

> Following the ways of the Father, he fashions material objects after his contemplation of their eternal Forms.[23]

Philo anticipates the language applied to Christ when he
speaks of this *Logos* from a platonizing viewpoint:

> As God is the first and only king of the universe, the
> way to him is rightly called the 'royal road.' Consider
> this road as philosophy ... the road taken by the
> ancient company of ascetics, who turned away from
> the entangling fascination of pleasure and devoted
> themselves to a noble and earnest cultivation of the
> beautiful. The Law names this royal road — which we
> call true philosophy — the Word and Spirit of God.[24]

To travel this road is for Philo equivalent to an initiation in
the Mysteries.[25] On it he will encounter the *Logos*, which is
for him the 'Son of God':

> I do not shrink from relating what has happened to
> me innumerable times. Often when I wished to put
> my philosophical thoughts in writing in my
> accustomed way, and saw quite clearly what was to
> be set down, I found my mind barren and rigid, so
> that I was obliged to give up without having
> accomplished anything, and seemed to be beset with
> idle fancies. At the same time I marvelled at the power
> of the reality of thought, with which it rests to open
> and close the womb of the human soul. At other
> times, however, I would begin empty and arrive,
> without any trouble, at fullness. Thoughts came flying
> like snowflakes or grains of corn invisibly from above,
> and it was as though divine power took hold of me
> and inspired me, so that I did not know where I was,
> who was with me, who I was, or what I was saying or
> writing; for then a flow of ideas was given me, a
> delightful clearness, keen insight, and lucid mastery of
> material, as if the inner eye were now able to see
> everything with the greatest clarity.[26]

Anyone can see from the mode of presentation of this 'road' that it leads to the consciousness, when the *Logos* is vitally active in him, of flowing in one current with the Divine. That is clear, too, in the following passage:

> When the spirit, moved by love, takes its flight into the holy of holies, soaring joyfully on divine wings, it forgets everything else and itself. It holds to and is filled only with the Power of which it is the follower and servant, and to this it offers the incense of the most sacred and chaste virtue.[27]

For Philo there are only two alternatives — to follow the way of the senses (perception and intellect), in which case one is confined in the limits of oneself and draws back from the cosmos; or to become aware of the universal Power and so, within one's own self, to experience the Eternal:

> He who wishes to escape from God falls into his own hands. For there are two things to be considered: the universal spirit, which is God; and one's own spirit. The latter flees to and takes refuge in the universal spirit, for one who goes out beyond his own spirit says to himself that it is nothing, and relates everything to God; but one who turns away from God discards him as First Cause, and makes himself the cause of everything that happens.[28]

In the platonic world-view, knowledge possesses an intrinsically religious character. It serves to bring the act of knowing into connection with the highest aspirations of human feeling — and only when it fulfils human desire completely does it rank, for Plato, as certain knowledge. It is then no longer representational or picture-making knowledge: it is an achieved reality of life.

Knowledge for Plato is a higher man within the external man, the essential man of whom the personal self is nothing more than a secondary image. Within man himself is born the transcendent, macrocosmic Man. And this brings us once more into the terrain of the Mystery-cults and their secret teachings, given a new form of expression in the platonic philosophy. We know of this secret doctrine from the report of Hippolytus, one of the Church Fathers. 'This is the great and ineffable Mystery of the Samothracians,' he says, referring to the guardians of a particular Mystery-cult:

> Only the initiates are permitted to know it. For in their Mysteries the Samothracians have the explicit tradition of a primordial, macrocosmic Man (Adam).[29]

The Mystery of love

It is also as an 'initiation' that we have to interpret the *Symposium* — the platonic 'Dialogue on Love.'

Love figures here as the herald of wisdom. We have seen that wisdom is the eternal *Logos,* the 'Son' of the eternal world-Father. To this *Logos* love stands in the position of a Mother. Before even so much as a spark of the light of wisdom can be struck in the human soul, there must be present in it an obscure urge or longing for the divine. Unconsciously it must draw man in the direction of what will subsequently, when it is raised into consciousness, constitute his highest bliss. Heraclitus apprehended the *daimon* in man; in Plato this is connected with the idea of love.

The *Symposium* comprises speeches on love from men of the most diverse social standing and attitudes to life: ordinary people, politicians and intellectuals are represented; and there is the comic poet Aristophanes and the tragic poet Agathon. In keeping with their different places in life, they all have a different experience and view of love. And from the way they express themselves, the level at which their *daimon* stands is made manifest. The role of love is to draw one being to another. The diversity of 'the many' into which the unified Godhead has poured itself out strives through love to return to unity and connectedness. Thus love is tinged with divinity. To understand it, one must also participate in the divine.

After people of several stages of maturity have expounded their notions of love, Socrates takes up the thread of the discourse and treats of love from the viewpoint of the knower. Love he denies to be a god — though it is something that leads man towards God. But love — *eros* — is not a divinity; for God is perfection, and contains the idea of the Beautiful and the Good, whereas *eros* is only a longing for the Beautiful and the Good. It occupies an intermediate position between man and God. It is a *daimon,* a being whose nature stands between the earthly and the heavenly.

It is a significant point that Socrates does not purport to give his own ideas on the subject of love, but only claims to recount what he received as a revelation from a woman — it is from the mantic art (divination) that he derives his conception of love. The priestess Diotima woke within Socrates the daimonic power which will lead him to the world of the divine. It was she who 'initiated' him, as we are told in a highly revealing passage of the *Symposium.* And now the question cannot be avoided: who is this 'wise woman' who woke the *daimon* in Socrates? She must certainly be more than a poetic fiction. No actual 'wise woman' on the perceptible place could have woken the *daimon* in his soul, however, since the power of awakening lies in the soul itself. It is in Socrates' own soul in fact that we must look for this 'wise woman.' At the same time there must be some reason why the one who raises the *daimon* in the soul into full reality should take on external, actual existence. It is because this power does not work as do the forces which are inherent in and native to the life of the soul itself. Evidently it is the soul-force which precedes the coming of wisdom that Socrates represents under the figure of a 'wise woman': the Mother-principle, which gives birth to Wisdom, the 'Son of God,' the *Logos.*

The 'Woman' stands for the power which is active unconsciously in the soul, which brings about the raising into
consciousness of the divine element in man. The soul, which
has not yet found wisdom, is the 'mother' of that experience
of divinization. Here we come to one of the central conceptions of Mystery-teaching, which acknowledges the human
soul as the mother of the god, leading man unconsciously
and with the inevitability of a natural force to his union with
the divine.[30]

All this casts light on the Mystery-interpretation of the
Greek myths. According to this, as we have seen, the world
of the gods is something generated in man's soul, and the
gods he beholds are images he has himself created. But then
he has to win through to a further understanding. He must
be able to take the divine creative power which is there in
himself — from which the images of the gods are derived —
and form that power itself into divine images, so that behind
the world of the gods he shapes an image of the divine
Mother. This is none other than the archetypal power of the
human soul.

Thus mythology places the goddesses alongside the male
gods. Our interpretation of this may be exemplified in the
study of the myths about Dionysus.[31]

Dionysus is the son of Zeus and a mortal mother, Semele.
But the mother is killed by lightning. Zeus, however, snat-
ches the still unformed child and allows it to grow within his
own thigh where it lies concealed. Hera, the mother of the
gods, stirs up the enmity of the Titans against Dionysus, and
they tear the child limb from limb. But Pallas Athene rescues
the still beating heart and brings it to Zeus. Out of it he
engenders his son for a second time.

The myth can be seen as representing a psychological
process of an extremely inward character. Let us interpret it
after the fashion of the Egyptian priest who instructed Solon
in the nature of myths.

It is related that Dionysus was born as the son of God and
a mortal mother, was dismembered and then reborn. This

has a fantastic ring to it, but the truth contained in the story is the birth of the divine and its subsequent destiny in individual human souls.[32] The divine is united with the soul, which is still subject to time and earthly conditions; and as soon as the god, the Dionysiac spirit, stirs within the soul, it experiences a longing for its real spiritual form. However, consciousness — again imaged as a female deity, Hera — appears and becomes jealous of the offspring from a qualitatively higher consciousness. She rouses the lower nature of man — the Titans — and the unformed divine child is dismembered. The divine knowledge exists in man only 'dismembered' by the understanding that is bound to the senses. If on the other hand there is within the man sufficient higher wisdom, this latter nurses and cherishes the unformed child until it is born again as a second son of God — Dionysus. And thus sense-derived understanding, the dismembered divine force in man, is reborn as the undivided wisdom which is identical with the *Logos*. It is the son of God and a mortal mother, who is the transitory human soul aspiring unconsciously after the divine.

We are still far removed from the spiritual reality which is played out in the myth if we recognize in it only psychological processes, and pictures of psychological events at that. This spiritual reality is not something which the soul experiences as confined to itself. It is rather released from itself to take part in a cosmic event. The reality of the myth is enacted not within but outside the soul.

Platonic philosophy is closely related to Greek myth, just as mysteriosophy is close to myth. Once begotten, the gods were the objects of external religious devotion. The story of their genesis was kept as a secret belonging to the Mysteries.

We can hardly be surprised that it was considered dangerous to betray the Mysteries: for it meant betraying the way the public divinities came into being. To those who understand it rightly, this is salutary knowledge; but destructive to those who do not.

5. From the Mysteries to Christianity

The Mysteries are crucial to fathoming the individual, the fate of the soul — in this world or the next — and the nature of community. Whereas Western religion has tended to stress the gulf between the individual and the transcendent God, the Mysteries existed to bridge over that metaphysical divide, to guide us to the divine within ourselves. Ideas concerning the fate of that divine self within us after earthly death already appear highly developed in ancient Egypt, and Steiner clearly recognized in the archaic texts of the priests the patterns of initiatory knowledge. More than just a hope for life in the hereafter, their beliefs were based upon the actual experience of being 'united with Eternity' as happened in all the Mysteries. We need more than ever to comprehend the source of those ideas nowadays, since otherwise the traditional notions of immortality and heaven will become ever more empty and unreal. Steiner also stresses how in the Mysteries the uncovering of the destiny of the individual was bound up with the whole community, including its dead. Nowadays sociologists have understood the value of ritual, without some form of which no society could continue. Steiner describes how in the Mithraic Mysteries, for example, the ritual forms and stages of initiation brought together a community on deeper levels of reality — and a rite from that source later reappears in Christianity, though transformed into a 'bloodless sacrifice' and communion. In comparing Christianity with further Eastern forms of initiation, Steiner brings out above all else how Christianity continued the Mystery knowledge in a form that brought it increasingly into the world of individual

From: *Das Christentum als mystische Tatsache*. Complete translation of the section *'Die ägyptische Mysterienweisheit.'*

believers. The drama of initiation had to descend into the world of event and history, and precisely through that drama the door to the inner reality of the Mysteries remained open.

The Egyptian Mysteries: the fate of the soul

The so-called 'Egyptian Book of the Dead,'* now restored to us by the diligence of nineteenth-century scholarship, demonstrates the existence among the ancient Egyptians of ideas concerning man's eternal existence and communion with the divine which might be summed up in the words attributed to Empedocles:

> When, set free from the body, released you rise to the
>   aether,
> You become divine, an immortal, escaped from the
>   power of death.

It contains, in fact, all kinds of teachings and invocations which were put into the grave along with the deceased in order to furnish him with a guide when he was released from the mortal state. By means of this literary work we can explore the most intimate ideas of the Egyptians concerning the eternal world and cosmogony.

The ideas of the gods which we find there remind us constantly of those familiar from the Greek Mysteries.[1] Osiris is a god who gradually came to be popular and was universally worshipped in Egypt, eclipsing the other local divinities and subsuming the attributes of the other gods into himself.[2] But whatever the ordinary people of Egypt thought about the nature of Osiris, in the 'Book of the Dead' we have evidence of a priestly doctrine, according to which Osiris was to be

*It has been called 'the greatest coherent literary work that has come down to us from ancient Egypt': R. Lipsius, *Das Totenbuch der alten Ägypter*, Berlin 1842, p.17.

found within the human soul. That emerges from everything said there about death and about the dead.

When the body is given over to the earth, preserved under earthly conditions, man's eternal part enters into the eternal condition which was in the beginning. It appears before Osiris. It stands before him for judgment, surrounded by the forty-two Judges of the Dead. The destiny of man's eternal being depends upon their verdict. If the soul has confessed its sins, it is deemed to be reconciled with the eternal Justice. Invisible powers then draw near and speak to it:

> Osiris N. has been purified in the pool which lies
> south of the Field of Hotep and north of the Field of
> Locusts, where the gods of verdure purify themselves
> at the fourth hour of the night and the eighth hour of
> the day, with the image of the heart of the gods,
> coming forth from night into day.[3]

This shows that in the world of eternal order, man's eternal nature has become Osiris: after the name Osiris stands the personal name of the deceased. Moreover, the one being united with eternity designates himself Osiris:

> I am the Osiris N. Growing under the blossoms of the
> fig-tree is the name of Osiris N.[4]

He has 'become an Osiris.'

Yet being an Osiris is nothing but the final, perfected stage of man's life and development. It is clear in this context that even Osiris in his cosmic role as a Judge is no more than a man who has attained to the stage of perfected existence. The difference between the human existence and divine existence is one of degree — and also of number. Behind this Mystery of the 'one and the many' lies the framework of ideas that belongs to the Mysteries.

Osiris in his cosmic form is a unitary being: hence he exists undivided in each human soul. Every man is an Osiris: yet the unitary Osiris has to be represented as a separate entity. Man is looked upon as being still in process of development, and at the end of the process comes his existence as a God. We should speak of a divinized condition of being, rather than of the independent existence of a Godhead, in the framework of Egyptian thought. Now it can hardly be doubted that in that framework of ideas no-one could be considered to attain Osirian existence when he crossed the threshold of eternity, unless he had already evolved to that level of being. Thus we must conclude that the highest mode of life that a man can lead is the transforming of oneself into an Osiris. To be truly man, one must already live the most perfect life of an Osiris that is possible under transitory conditions. Human perfection means living like an Osiris — means undergoing all that Osiris underwent.

It is in this way that the Osiris-myth takes on its deeper dimension of meaning, becoming the paradigm of life for the man who wants to awaken eternal being within himself.[5] Osiris is torn to pieces by Typhon; he is killed. The members of his body are cherished and cared for by his consort, Isis. After his death, he caused a ray of light to fall upon her and she bore his son, Horus, who then takes over the earthly tasks of Osiris: he is the second, still immature Osiris — but he is in process of becoming an Osiris in the full sense. This true Osiris is to be found in the human soul. For although the soul is to begin with connected to the transitory realm, it is destined to give birth to the eternal. Man may therefore be termed the tomb of Osiris; it is man's lower nature — Typhon or Set — which has killed him. The love which is present in his soul — Isis — must cherish and care for the members of his corpse, and then the higher nature or eternal soul — Horus — can be born, and in due course rise to the state of 'being an Osiris.'

This then is the 'initiation' practised in Egypt. It taught that the man who aspires to the highest stage of being must recapitulate in himself microcosmically the universal, macrocosmic events connected with Osiris. Plato has described such a cosmic process: the Creator had stretched out the world-soul on the world-body in the form of a cross, and the subsequent organization of the cosmos constitutes a redemption of the crucified world-soul.[6] If a man is to 'become an Osiris' the same process must take place in miniature. The initiand must allow his inner experience of 'becoming an Osiris' to unfold and fuse with the events of the cosmic Osirian myth.

If we were able to look inside the temples where the initiatory 'transformation into Osiris' took place, we would see that the events enacted there on the human scale were a representation of the cosmogony. Man originates from the 'Father,' and is to bear in himself the Son; the actual presence within him of the divinity, held captive by a spell, is to be brought to manifestation. The god in him is held down by the power of earthly nature: that lower nature must become a grave, from which the higher nature can rise to new life. The information we possess about the scenarios of initiation makes sense when we understand this.[7] People were sub-jected to procedures whose character was mysterious, but which were intended to 'kill' the earthly and awaken some-thing higher. Further detail is not needed here, for we com-prehend the intention behind these procedures.

The intention was that every one who had undergone initiation would be able to make a 'confession.' Every initiate could declare that he had seen hovering before him the prospect of infinity, reaching up to the divine; that he had felt within him also the power of the divine, and had laid to rest in the tomb all that held down that power; he had died to earthly things; he was indeed dead, for as a lower man he had died, and had been in the underworld among the dead — that is, with those who are already united with eternity; after his sojourn in the netherworld he had risen again from the dead, but as another, no longer as one belonging to transitory nature; all that is transitory was absorbed into the all-permeating *Logos,* and he belonged henceforth among those who live for ever at the right hand of Osiris; he will himself become a true Osiris, united with eternal order, and the power of judgment over life and death will be put in his hand. The initiand had to undergo whatever experience was necessary in order for him to make such a 'confession' — an experience of a most exalted kind.[8]

If these experiences came to the attention of the uninitiated, however, it is easy to see that he would comprehend nothing of what actually took place in the soul of the neophyte. He would take the latter's death, burial and resurrection as a physical occurrence, and the spiritual realities of a higher existential plane would take on the appearance of an event contradicting the whole natural order of things: a miracle. And in that sense, a miracle is what initiation was.

The Soul and the Community: the Mysteries of Mithras

The Mithraic Mysteries played an important role at the time of Christian origins, spreading over the first centuries far into western Europe.[9] To grasp the spirit of these Mysteries, it must be recognized that they were founded on a set of presuppositions which for the world of Antiquity were perfectly justified, and continued to be so up to the time of the Mystery of Golgotha. The Mithraic Mysteries depended on the idea that a human society (whether an ethnic group or some smaller division within an ethnic grouping) comprised more than the separate atomic components called individual men. Such communities, if they were to have any grounding in reality, must be thought of as possessing a living spirit, a supersensible being that lived in them as a collective or communal spirit. A society of so-and-so-many heads was more than the sum of its members: the peoples of Antiquity regarded society as the creation, even as the embodiment, of the actively present spirit of the community. To take a living part in this spirit, to share in the thoughts of this communal

From *Bausteine zu einer Erkenntnis des Mysteriums von Golgatha*, extract from lecture 9.

mind was the goal of those who were received into these Mysteries.[10]

The aim was not at all to stand outside society so as to pursue one's own obstinately egoistic ideas, feelings or impulses of will, but to live in such a way as to let the ideas of the common spirit play in. The Mithraic Mysteries above all stood for the view that this cannot be achieved so long as society is looked on as if it consisted of no more that is outwardly present, which in truth rather overshadows and obscures the spirit of the community. The context of social life, according to them, includes also the dead. Hence the more we can commune with those long dead, the better we shall order our present life. Indeed, it seemed best to commune with the spirits of those longest dead, going back to the first ancestor of the tribe, community or family to establish a psychic connection. For the dead soul had advanced to a higher state by passing through the gates of death, and had a better knowledge of what was taking place on earth even than those still in earthly life in the body. The whole aim of the Mithraic Mysteries was to put the neophyte, by means of cultic and other actions, in touch with the souls of the dead.

A first stage, obligatory for all who entered the Mysteries, was characterized by the name of a bird: a raven. A Raven (corax) was an initiate of the first grade. The point of the Mystery-rites, of the powerful symbols and the dramatic enactments to which he was subjected, was to enable him to transcend what he merely saw with his eyes all around him, or what he learned in common with his fellow men, and to commune with the thoughts of the dead. It was a kind of remembering of the dead, which became a faculty that could be deepened and extended.

A Raven had the duty of not sleeping; he was to be constantly alert to the moment, his eyes wide open. In this way he could serve the needs of his fellow men, and also become familiar with the events of nature. No-one of a sleepy disposition, or who had no perception of man and nature, qualified for admittance to the Mysteries. For a proper interest in life in the outer world was what fitted a person for the tasks to be fulfilled in the Mysteries, which were to share in the diversity of life-experiences, to enter into the joys and the sufferings of the world and things which were happening. Apathy in the face of world-events was of no value. For the Raven had the initial task of reproducing, of recreating within the Mysteries, what he had experienced in the world. His experiences thereby became a channel of communication with the dead for whom he was seeking.*

One might think that a higher grade initiate would have been better fitted to this task. But it was not so. A *mystes* of the first grade was suited to it precisely because he still possessed all the feelings of sympathy and antipathy that belong to outer life in the world, whereas the higher grades demanded renunciation of these to a greater or lesser extent. Hence it was for the Ravens to carry over into the Mysteries what they experienced, still in a more or less worldly fashion; and to mediate between the world and those who died long before.

When someone was ripe for initiation into the second grade,[11] he became a genuine student of secret knowledge, an Occultist (*kryphios*) as we would call him today.[12] He was now ready not only to convey information from the outside world to the Mysteries, but also to receive communications from the side of the dead. This world of the dead was a quite concrete reality beyond that of the senses, from which came impulses for action in the external world.

To be considered ready for the third grade, the pupil had to become an integral part of the spiritual order which

---

* Legend preserves something of this. (I have often pointed out the profound basis of the majority of legends.) Legend tells that Friedrich Barbarossa, long after he died, was given information by the ravens in his mountain tomb. Or again, Charlemagne on the Untersberg in Salzburg is surrounded by ravens who tell him about what is happening in the outside world. These are echoes of the Mysteries, with specifically Mithraic affinities.

stretches from the supersensible down to the external world, where it comes into contact with the reality of the senses. He was then in a position to make use of what he had taken up from the inner sanctum of the Mysteries. This singled him out as a Soldier (*miles*), a fighter for all that was revealed from the world beyond the senses to the sensible world.

Now it may seem extremely unfair that the majority of the people were left to languish in ignorance, and only a few individuals were initiated into these most important matters. But there is more to it than that, as you will understand if you consider what I said earlier on: the people considered themselves in mind and soul as a group, and they were content that a few individuals should act because they did so on behalf of the group. They had no sense of individuality, but were members of the group. In an age of unselfconscious belonging, of living wholly in the shared soul of the community, it was a natural way of proceeding.

After a period as a Soldier, fighting for the spiritual world, the initiate was considered ready to establish smaller groups within the community. Such organizations are needed within a larger group. In Antiquity, individuals did not simply take it upon themselves to found an association; that would not have worked. To organize an association in the Mithraic Mysteries there had to be someone initiated to the fourth grade: a Lion (*leo*) as he was called. It had to be someone grounded in the spiritual life, who was able to unite the sources of activity stemming not only from the living, but also from the dead.

After the fourth grade, the *mystes* rose to higher levels by means of certain procedures, enabling him to take over the leadership of already existing groups — an ethnic group, including within it also the dead of that community. If we go back to the period eight, nine or ten centuries before the Christian epoch we would find conditions bearing little resemblance to modern times. No-one then would have thought of choosing arbitrarily the leaders of the community. If something had to be done in connection with the community as a whole, there had to be an initiate of the fifth grade: a Persian *(perses)*.[13]

Further progress in the Mysteries led to the knowledge of the dawning Sun-mystery in the human soul.[14] Finally, there was the seventh grade. It is not my intention to pursue these matters further. I wished to characterize the progress of the initiate, and the way in which his spiritual knowledge was at the same time a capacity to work in the wider community.

It is obvious and inevitable that the further development of humanity has meant that the stage of shared-soul experience had to be left behind. Gradually, people began to have a direct experience of the ego, consciously grasping their individuality. This had been prepared over many centuries; but the breakthrough, the crisis in this sphere, came at the time of the Mystery of Golgotha.

Now the real initiates of the Mystery teachings were aware that, while it was possible for people to attain all kinds of psychic experiences, in this one respect they were entirely dependent on the Mysteries: it was only in the Mysteries that there existed any concrete understanding of the ego, anything beyond mere abstract ideas. Other spiritual and psychic experiences were accessible to humanity, but the ego had to be nurtured through the techniques of the Mysteries, which gave its development the powerful stimulation it needed. This was an essential aspect of the initiates' knowledge.

Then came the time for Christianity. And, as you know, evolving Christianity formed a kind of alliance with the Roman *imperium*. (I have described elsewhere how this alliance came about.) As a result of this alliance, the Church became anxious to suppress any knowledge of previous spiritual history, such as I have mentioned, and as far as possible prevent any information about it coming down to posterity. The Mystery-rites continued, in some cases well on into the Christian era, to bring man into contact — whether in the body or out of the body — with those divine powers which fostered his ego-consciousness. But all this the Church resolved to suppress. If we want to attain a deeper comprehension of how Christianity developed in this context, we must not limit our view solely to the emergence of dogma, but consider also the history of cultic practices. From some points of view, the history of the cult has far more importance than that of the articles of faith. Dogma is an endless source of controversy, which rises phoenix-like from its own ashes again and again; no matter how thoroughly a point of dogma is laid to rest, some eccentric is always likely to pop up, championing the outmoded point of view. Cults are far easier to eradicate. The ancient rites, which were in a sense the external signs and symbols for the inner processes of the Mysteries, were rooted out so as to make it impossible to decipher from the surviving cultic practices how they had brought people close to the divine-spiritual powers.

We get to the heart of the matter if we turn to consider briefly the Christian liturgy — for instance, the central cultic act of the Catholic Church, the sacrifice of the Mass. It has an extremely profound meaning, and it is, with all that is related to it, a continuation and development of the Mithraic Mysteries, combined with certain elements of the Eleusinian Mysteries. The sacrifice of the Mass and many of the ceremonies associated with it is simply a further development of the ancient cults. There has been some alteration: the sanguinary character which the Mithraic Mysteries had gradually assumed has been codified, it is true.[15] But the agreement in countless details between the two and the common spirit which unites them is hard to overlook. One aspect of the rite — the fact that the priest as well as the communicant has to fast for a certain period before receiving the 'body of Christ' — tells us far more that is essential to our understanding than many of the things that were fiercely debated in the Middle Ages. This is just one example. And if (as may happen) the priest neglects the order to fast before celebrating the eucharist, the transubstantiation and communion lose their meaning and the effect they are suppose to have. The effect is largely lost, too, if the communicants have not been properly instructed. It can be efficacious only if suitable instruction has been given to the candidate about what he will experience upon receiving the 'bloodless sacrifice' of the 'body of Christ.' But we all know how little attention is paid to these subtleties nowadays. It is scarcely realized that there ought to be an actual experience — an inner intimation which would represent a renewal under modern conditions of the stimulus received by those in the Mithraic Mysteries. Genuine 'Mysteries' do indeed underlie the forms of the Christian cult, behind the scenes of history. And with the ordination of priests, the Church attempted to establish a kind of continuation of the ancient principle of initiation. The Church has for the most part forgotten, however, that the principle of initiation consisted in giving instruction on the way to respond to certain experiences.

The life of a initiate: Buddha and Christ

Anyone who wished to comprehend what initiation meant had to awaken in himself the powers enabling him to adopt a higher stance, on a new existential plane. It required a premeditated course of life, leading to such a higher experience. And though in each individual case these experiences might come about in various ways, it always happens that we can point to specific, typical forms. The life of an initiate has a typical character, which can be described without reference to the particular personality concerned.

To put it another way: an individual could be described as treading the path to divinization only if he had undergone the particular typical experiences of an initiate. One example is the Buddha as seen by his disciples; and as such a one did Jesus first appear in his own society. We know today of the parallelism between the biographies of the Buddha and Jesus. One has only to observe the detailed correspondences

From: 'Die ägyptische Mysterienweisheit' in Das Christentum als mystische Tatsache.

between them to realize that any attempt at denial would be vain.*

There is an annunciation of Buddha's birth to Queen Maya by a white elephant, which overshadows her and tells her that she is to bring forth a 'divine man.' 'And he will attune all beings to love and friendship, and will unite them in a bond of religious fervour.' Compare with this the passage from the Gospel of Luke where an angel is sent:

> to a virgin pledged to be married to a man named Joseph, a descendant of David. The virgin's name was Mary. The angel went to her and said, 'Greetings, you who are highly favoured! ... You will be with child and give birth to a son, and you are to give him the name Jesus. He will be great and will be called the Son of the Most High.'

The Brahmans (Indian priests) understand the meaning of the birth of a Buddha. They interpret Maya's dream according to a totally schematic concept of what a Buddha is: the individual's life must correspond to this concept exactly. Similarly we find in the Gospel of Matthew that Herod:

> called together all the people's chief priests and teachers of the law, and asked them where the Christ was to be born.

One of the Brahmans, Asita, says of the Buddha:

> This child is the one who will become a Buddha, the saviour, the leader to immortality, freedom and the light.

Compare with this what happens in the Gospel of Luke:

---

* See the convincing account in Seydel, Rudolf, *Buddha und Christus*, Breslau 1884, especially pp.8–14.[15a]

Now there was a man in Jerusalem called Simeon,
who was righteous and devout. He was waiting for
the consolation of Israel, and the Holy spirit was upon
him ... When the parents brought in the child Jesus to
do for him what the custom of the Law required,
Simeon took him in his arms and praised God, saying:
Lord, as you have promised you now dismiss your
servant in peace. For my eyes have seen your
salvation, which you have prepared in the sight of all
people, a light for revelation to the Gentiles, and for
glory to your people Israel.

Tradition reports of the Buddha that when he was a child of
twelve he went missing, and was found again under a tree,
surrounded by the poets and sages of the time. Correspondingly we find in the Gospel of Luke:

Every year his parents went up to Jerusalem for the
Feast of the Passover. When he was twelve years old,
they went up to the Feast, according to the custom.
After the feast was over, while his parents were
returning home, the boy Jesus stayed behind in
Jerusalem, but they were unaware of it. Thinking that
he was in their company, they travelled on for a day.
Then they began looking for him among their relatives
and friends. When they did not find him, they went
back to Jerusalem to look for him. After three days
they found him in the Temple, sitting among the
teachers, listening to them and asking questions.
Everyone who heard him was amazed at his
understanding and his answers.

The Buddha withdrew into solitude, and when he returned
a virgin greeted him with words of benediction: 'Blessed are
the mother, the father and the wife to whom you belong.'
But he answered: 'Only those are blessed who have reached
nirvana.' The reference is to those who have entered the

world of the eternal order of things. Compare in the Gospel of Luke:

> As Jesus was saying these things, a woman in the crowd called out, 'Blessed is the mother who gave you birth and the breasts which fed you!' He replied, 'Blessed rather are those who hear the word of God and obey it.'

At one point in his life, the Tempter (Mara) comes to Buddha and promises him all the kingdoms of the earth. The Buddha rejects it all with the words: 'I know well that I am destined to have a kingdom, but I do not desire an earthly one; I will achieve enlightenment and make all the world rejoice.' Mara has to admit, 'My power is at an end.' Jesus responds to the same temptation, saying:

> 'Away from me, Satan! For it is written: Worship the Lord your god, and serve him only.'
> Then the devil left him ...

The parallels could be documented at considerably greater length, all pointing in the same direction.

The Buddha's life comes to a sublime ending. Whilst on a journey, he felt ill. He came to the river Hiranya, near Kusinagara, and there he lay down on a rug spread for him by his beloved disciple Ananda. His body began to shine from within. He died transfigured, as a body of light, saying 'Nothing is permanent.' This death of the Buddha corresponds to the Transfiguration of Jesus:

> About eight days after Jesus said this, he took Peter, John and James with him and went up on to a mountain to pray. As he was praying, the appearance of his face changed, and his clothes became as bright as a flash of lightning.

The Buddha's earthly life ends at this juncture. But in the life of Jesus this is just the beginning of the most important part — his suffering, death and resurrection. The difference between the Buddha and Christ is shown in the necessity for the life of Christ Jesus to continue beyond the furthest point of the Buddha's life.* Buddha and Christ cannot be comprehended simply by lumping everything together.

The correspondence between these two redemptive lives leads unambiguously to the conclusion, already indicated by the narratives themselves, that when the priests or sages hear what kind of birth has occurred they know already what is involved. They have to do with a 'divine man,' and they know what course of life the personality must adopt so that it shall correspond to what they know of such a 'divine man.' Mysteriosophy contains the eternal prototype for such a course in life, which he must and can only fulfil. It is like a law of nature, and as the properties of a chemical are exactly determined, a Buddha or Christ must live a precisely determined life. Their lives are not narrated to reveal the accidents of biography, but rather to show the typical features, defined by mysteriosophy for all ages to come.

The legend of the Buddha is no more a biography in the ordinary sense than the Gospels are supposed to be such a biography of Christ Jesus. Neither is concerned with contingent events, but rather with the prototypical life of a world-redeemer. The model for both accounts is not external, physical happenings but the traditional teachings of the Mysteries. For those who recognize their divine nature, the Buddha and Jesus are essentially 'initiates':† their lives are raised above everything transitory, and what is known about the nature of the initiated must be applicable to them. The contingencies of their lives are not narrated, but one says of

* This will be demonstrated further below. Other versions of the death of the Buddha do not concern us here, of profound interest though they may be from other points of view.

† Jesus is an 'initiate' in the sense that the Christ-being is present in him.[15b]

them, 'In the beginning was the Word, and the Word was with God, and the Word was a God ... And the Word became flesh and dwelt among us.'

Yet the life of Jesus transcends the life of the Buddha. The Buddha's life ends with his transfiguration, whereas the most significant part of Jesus' life begins after the Transfiguration. Translated into the terms of initiation, the Buddha reached the point at which the divine light begins to shine in man, standing on the verge of earthly life and becoming one with the light of the world. Jesus goes further: he does not physically die at the moment when the light of the world shines through him. At that moment he is a Buddha; but at the same time he enters upon a higher stage of initiation, that of suffering and death. And when his earthly part is lost to view, the spiritual light, the light of the world, does not go out but leads on to his resurrection. To his followers he is revealed to be the Christ.

As soon as he achieves his 'transfiguration,' the Buddha is lost in the all-pervading blissful life of the spirit. Christ-Jesus, however, re-kindles the all-pervading spirit once more to life in the form of present human existence. Something like this had been achieved by the initiates in the higher stages of the Mysteries.[16] But there it had had a mythical image-character. The initiates of Osiris experienced a 'resurrection' on the level of image-consciousness. In the life of Christ, initiation in the 'Great Mysteries' was added to the stage of Buddha-initiation, not, however, on the plane of mythological images but as a real event. The life of the Buddha demonstrated that man is in essence the divine *Logos* (Word): when his earthly part perishes, man returns to the *Logos,* to the light. But in Jesus, the *Logos* takes on existence as an actual man, the Word becomes flesh. The ritual pattern enacted by the Mystery-cults of the ancient world in the secrecy of their temple precincts was grasped by Christianity in an event of world history. Christ Jesus appeared in his own time as an initiate — but one initiated in a uniquely great way. He was a proof of the divine presence in the world. Henceforth for

the Christian community, mysteriosophy would be indissolubly bound up with the personality of Christ Jesus. The
fact that he had lived, and that those who acknowledge him
are 'his own,'[17] now constituted a belief that was able to take
the place of the Mysteries and their practices. From then on,
part of what had formerly been attainable only through the
techniques of the Mysteries was accessible to the Christian
communities through their conviction that God had shown
himself in the presence of the Word among them.

The long preparation required for each individual was no
longer the sole way to the spirit. To it had to be added the
witness to the deeds and words of Jesus which had been
handed down:

> That which was from the beginning, which we have
> heard, which we have seen with our eyes, which we
> have looked on and our hands have touched — this
> we proclaim concerning the Word of life ... We
> proclaim to you what we have seen and heard, so that
> you also may have fellowship with us.[18]

That sense of immediate presence is to be a bond of living
union for all generations and all peoples, embracing them all
mystically in a universal Church. Hence we understand the
declaration of Augustine:

> I would not believe the message of the gospel, if I
> were not urged to do so by the authority of the
> Catholic Church.[19]

The Gospels do not carry weight as statements or truth in
themselves. They are to be believed because they are grounded in the personal presence of Jesus, and because the
Church in a mysterious way draws from that personal
presence its power to make the truth manifest.

The Mysteries handed down the techniques of coming to
the truth. The Christian *ecclesia* propagates this truth in itself.

The Mysteries had fostered a trust in the spiritual powers which were awakened in man's inner nature through initiation. To this was added the trust in the Founder, the Initiator as such. The Mysteries had been a process of the divinization of man — and actual experience of being made God.[20] Jesus attained oneness with God: therefore one must cling to him, so as to share in his divinization as part of the community which he founded. That is the Christian claim.

The divinization of Jesus has a universal significance, in which the community of his faithful can share:

> See, I am with you always, to the very end of the world.[21]

The birth in Bethlehem bears the stamp of an eternal reality. Hence when the birth of Jesus is mentioned in the Christmas antiphon, it is said to happen every Christmastime:

> *Hodie Christus natus est, hodie Salvator apparuit,*
> *Hodie in Terra canunt Angeli, laetantur Archangeli, ...*

'Today Christ is born, today the Saviour has appeared, today the angels sing on earth, the archangels rejoice ... '

The Christ-experience, then, was a specific stage of initiation.[22] In pre-Christian times the *mystai* attained to this stage of Christianization, but they were then in a state of spiritual vision in the higher worlds, to which there was nothing equivalent among the facts of the sense-world. The inner meaning of the Mystery of Golgotha was experienced spiritually. When the Christian initiates achieve this stage of initiation, however, they behold at that very moment the historical event on Golgotha. And they know that in the event which took place, in the sense-perceptible world, is contained the spiritual content which had been enacted supersensibly in the Mysteries.

In the Mystery-places the spirit had been poured out upon the *mystai* of old. Through the 'Mystery of Golgotha' it was poured out upon the whole Christian community. There was still a place for initiation. For whereas faith allows a person to participate unconsciously in the content of the Mysteries of Golgotha, initiation leads to a fully conscious connection with the power which streams invisibly from the events depicted in the New Testament, and which ever since then has pervaded spiritually the life of humanity.[23]

6. The Apocalypse of John

The last book of the Bible is a Mystery in many senses, from its authorship to the riddling sense of its many prophecies. What it shares with the Mysteries proper is especially the theme of transformation — indeed of dramatic, overwhelming change. But it is universal change, engulfing whole societies and dramatizing opposing cultural values ('Babylon', 'Jerusalem'). It is addressed to typical Communities (groups of people, not the organizational entities or even building-centred implications of the conventional rendering 'Church'). It has provided the basis for many social visions, sometimes of an apparently secular nature such as Marxism which still preserves many structures of apocalypse in its prophecy of the inevitable, all-transforming revolution. Once cut loose, indeed, from the foundations of spiritual experience to which it alludes, the Apocalypse has become one of the greatest speculative fantasies in the history of thought. Attempts to relate it to history become an illusory guessing-game, and efforts to actualize its images in the immediacy of a personal life may release revolutionary energies whose tendency is as likely to be destructive as renovatory. Steiner's interpretation restores the Apocalypse to its link with the Mysteries, and the implications go far beyond the exegetical. For it puts the transformation of the individual back at the heart of a collective, social and even cosmic process of renewal. Lose that central thread, and a change in society will inevitably sweep away individuals and individuals' rights; if we do not transform people from within, there will be no alternative but to change them violently and to cling on to power by further violence, as twentieth century history shows. Social change demands that certain individuals carry burdens and even suffer for what they wish to bring about. Strangely, even Jung failed to recognize that this apocalyptic suffering is positive and worthwhile, both for the individual's higher development and for the world. Real change requires that individuals deepen their sufferings in order to show the way forward — a new form of the Mystery-process which Steiner found marvellously depicted here.

The seven letters

I

At the end of the New Testament stands an extraordinary document. It is the Apocalypse — the secret revelation of Saint John. The esoteric character of the work is apparent from the opening words:

> The revelation of Jesus the Christ, which God granted
> him in order to show to his servants how the
> necessary events will shortly run their course. This is
> communicated in signs sent by God's angel to his
> servant John.[1]

The revelation is imparted 'in signs': we must not therefore interpret the text literally, but look for a deeper meaning which is signified by the external sense. Nor is this all that points us to a 'hidden meaning.'

John addresses seven churches in Asia Minor. This cannot mean actually existing communities. Rather, the number seven is a sacred symbol and must have been chosen because of what it represents — there must in reality have been a number of other communities in Asia. Moreover, the way in which John receives the revelation equally suggests an esoteric significance:

From: *Das Christentum als mystische Tatsache.*

> I was in the spirit on the Lord's Day, and I heard
> behind me a voice like a trumpet saying, 'Write what
> you see in a book and send it to the Seven
> Communities.'[2]

He received the revelation when he was 'in the spirit.' Also,
it is a revelation of Jesus the Christ, presenting in esoteric
form the meaning of Christ Jesus' manifestation to the world.

Therefore we are to look for the hidden meaning of the
Apocalypse in the teaching of Christ — so that the revelation
it contains stands in the same relation to mainstream Christianity as the Mysteries in pre-Christian times stood to the
public religion. This would seem to justify us in approaching
the Apocalypse as a Mystery.[3]

What then does the Apocalypse mean by addressing the
Seven Communities? To understand it, we must take a
specific instance from the seven messages, and we may begin
with the first one:

> Write to the angel of the community in Ephesus: These
> are the words of him who holds the seven stars in his
> right hand, and who walks among the seven golden
> lights: I know your deeds, and what you have suffered
> and also your patient endurance, and that you will not
> support those who are evil; also, that you have called
> to account those who call themselves apostles and are
> not, and that you have recognized them as false. And
> you are enduring patiently and are building up your
> work upon my name, and you have not grown weary.
> But I demand of you that you should attain the highest
> love: consider from what you have fallen, change your
> way of thinking, and achieve the highest deeds. Other-
> wise, I will come to you and remove your light from
> its place — unless you change your way of thinking.
>
> But this you have, that you despise the ways of the
> Nicolaitans, which I too despise.
>
> He who has ears to hear what the Spirit says to the

> Communities, let him hear: 'To the victor I will give
> food from the Tree of Life, which stands in the
> Paradise of God.'[4]

Such is the message to the angel of the first Community. The 'angel' is to be understood as the spirit of the community. The angel has entered upon the direction indicated by Christianity, and is able to distinguish between the true and false professors of Christian belief. He wishes to work in a Christian way, founded upon 'the name of Christ.'

But he is urged not to fall short of the 'highest love' through lapsing into any sort of error. He is shown the possibility of going astray through such errors. The way to the divine has been revealed through Christ Jesus: perseverance is needed in order to press forward in the original spirit of the movement. Otherwise it is possible to rest content with one's understanding of Christ too soon, as is the case if one is led a certain way but then abandons this guidance for erroneous fixed ideas about it; one then falls back upon the lower self in human nature. This is the failure to attain to one's 'highest love.' The knowledge derived from the senses and the intellect is to be exalted, spiritualized and made divine by becoming wisdom, on a higher plane: if it is not, it remains on the level of the transitory.

Christ Jesus has pointed out the path to the Eternal. Knowledge must be tirelessly led along the path which leads to its becoming 'divine knowledge.' In the spirit of love it must pursue the traces which will lead to its becoming 'wisdom.'

The Nicolaitans were a sect which did not fully grasp the meaning of Christianity.[5] They saw only that Christ is the divine Word, the eternal Wisdom which comes to birth in man. They therefore identified human wisdom and divine Word, supposing that the pursuit of human knowledge was the realization of the divine in the world. But Christian wisdom cannot be construed in this way. Knowledge, or human wisdom, is as perishable as everything else if it does not undergo that transformation into 'divine wisdom.'[6] You, however, says the Spirit to the angel at Ephesus, have not relied in this way upon mere human wisdom. You have persevered in the path of Christianity. Yet to reach the goal you need nothing short of the first and highest love. You need a love greater than all other loves, because only then can it be the 'first love.' The road to the divine reaches endlessly before you and the first step, once gained, is the starting point for an ascent that leads ever higher.

So must we understand the message to the first of the Communities, and it must serve as an example for the rest.[7]

II

These utterances in the language of apocalyptic are able to lead those who unveil them deep into the imaginative world of the Mysteries. For what did the Apocalyptist wish to write — what did he wish to represent? To answer the question we must refer briefly to the origin of the Apocalypse. Where do we first find the contents of the Apocalypse?

If you could look back into the Mysteries of ancient Greece — into the Orphic and Eleusinian Mysteries — if you could go back into the Mysteries of ancient Egypt, Mesopotamia, Persia or India, you would find the Apocalypse everywhere. It existed, it was there: not in written form, but livingly transmitted from one generation of priests to another. Down the generations of the hierophants memory was so potent that it could master the extensive material. One need only remember the epic singers of the *Iliad*, who travelled about reciting from memory; and even in much later times memory was far better than ours, and has deteriorated significantly in quite recent times. In the Mysteries, truths were not written down but lived on from generation to generation of the hierophants.

Why then was the Apocalypse written down?

From *Die Apokalypse des Johannes* (lectures 1908; GA no. 104), extracts from lectures 12 and 2.

It was intended to serve as a book of instruction for those who were bringing pupils to the stage of initiation. One who was initiated at that period was led out of the physical body, and lay as if dead; but in that condition the hierophant enabled him to see spiritually in his etheric body. Later, through the impetus given to human evolution by the Christ, the initiate would be able to see spiritually while still in the physical body. In that sense the ancient initiates were prophets of Christ, and actually pointed the way to his coming. They were able to do so because Christ in this Apocalypse is a figure who is yet to come, in the future. The Mystery of Golgotha had not yet taken place — a Mystery in which the whole drama of initiation was lived through historically by a person in the physical body.[8]

Where then could we look for an understanding of the Mystery of Golgotha? At one stage, the initiates had comprehended it in an out-of-the-body state. The reality of what took place on Golgotha was on another level of consciousness. The Event of Golgotha could have taken place before thousands of people, and yet it would have passed them by unnoticed. For what would it have been to them? Just the death of an ordinary condemned person! To understand the reality of Golgotha was only possible when the contents of the Mysteries were known. The hierophants would then be able to say to their pupils that if they used the knowledge granted to them in the Mysteries, they would recognize the one whom they had seen during the three-and-a-half-day sleep, the one foretold by the prophets. The Apocalyptist was one who had received the oral tradition of the Mysteries, and said: When I am filled with all that comes to me from the Mysteries, there appears to me — the Christ.[9]

Thus the Apocalypse was nothing new. What was new was its application to the unique historical event of Golgotha. That was the essential point: for those with ears to hear, the Apocalypse of John could unveil a real understanding of the Mystery of Golgotha. That was the intention of its author.

The Apocalypse came down to him, then, from the ancient

Mysteries as one of the ancient sacred books of mankind. But outwardly it has been presented to the world by 'the Disciple whom the Lord loved,' the one whom the Lord charged with the task of proclaiming his true nature. He is the 'one who is to remain until Christ comes.'[10] Hence those who have illumined consciousness will understand him, for he is the great teacher of the reality of the Event of Golgotha and has given to mankind the means by which it can truly be understood.

The writer says at the beginning of the Apocalypse – and I shall translate the first words in order to bring out their actual sense:

> The revelation of Jesus the Christ, which God granted
> him in order to show to his servants in brief the
> events which must necessarily run their course. This is
> communicated in signs sent by God's angel to his
> servant John.

He is the one who wrote them down. Now what does he mean by 'in brief'?* He means that if he were to describe the whole future development of the earth from now onward to its goal, he would have to write an enormous amount; this is only a short sketch. The translators who have not caught the spirit of the Apocalypse rendered it as 'events which must shortly come about,' as if what the Apocalypse describes were about to happen in the immediate future! But it really means 'to show in brief' what will take place. It is not to be wondered at that of all Christian documents this one has been the most misunderstood, for it contains nothing less than a great part of the Mysteries of Christianity. It contains what we may designate the profoundest 'esoteric Christianity.'[11]

---

* I have shown that the original text admits of this interpretation in my 'Introduction' to *Bilder okkulter Siegel und Säulen. Der Münchener Kongress 1907*, Dornach 1975.

Yet almost from the very beginnings of the Christian spiritual movement it has been misunderstood by all who were not actually in the ranks of the Christian initiates. The way in which it has been misread has itself varied with the times, in accordance with the great diversity of thought and culture. It was misread at times of materialism in spiritual matters, misread at the times of fanaticism and rivalry between the great religious movements, misread especially in modern times when it is assumed that the riddle of the universe could be solved in sense-bound and grossly materialistic terms.

High spiritual truths were proclaimed at the outset of the Christian movement to those able to understand them. In so far as they can be put into writing, they are disclosed in the Apocalypse of John — the so-called 'canonical' Revelation.[12] But even in the earliest Christian times, the exoteric party was little inclined to understanding the deeper spiritual meaning of esoteric Christianity. That is how it came about that in the earliest period of Christianity the exoteric party considered the great events of cosmic spiritual evolution — seen in visions and understood by those with spiritual sight — were things about to be played out on the material plane in the life of the times. That is how it came about that those who could comprehend only the exoteric meaning of what the author of the Apocalypse described from the results of his initiation, came to the conclusion that processes extending over thousands of years, described by the great visionary, were external and visible happenings about to take place in the near future before their very eyes. They thought that the writer was predicting the return of Christ Jesus in the immediate future from the physical and perceptible clouds ...[13]

To anyone with a grounding in spiritual science, however, it will no doubt be obvious from the very opening words what the Apocalypse really purports to be. And we may note that the one from whom its contents stem finds himself in an island solitude, enveloped by the sacred atmosphere of one of the ancient holy places of the Mysteries. It is said too that the one who gives us the Apocalypse 'was in the spirit' — he perceived it spiritually.[14] This proves that the content of the Apocalypse stems from a higher mode of consciousness, attained by means of a creative evolution of the soul: an initiation. What cannot be seen or heard with physical senses in the physical world is given a form in the so-called 'secret revelation' of John, so that through Christianity it can be communicated to the world.

Thus it is a representation of an initiation, a Christian initiation. We need for the moment only consider briefly what initiation is, placing it fleetingly before our souls. The question of what actually happens in initiation will occupy us at length as we penetrate deeper into the substance of the Apocalypse. But first we can make a rough sketch in broad outline, and afterwards get down to painting the detail ... [15]

At first it is as though a person were speaking behind a screen. You hear the sound of his voice but cannot see him. It is like that with perception of the spiritual world. It appears first in pictures; then sounds are heard; and then the last veil falls away, as if we were to take away the screen behind which the man is speaking and we see the man himself — we see the spiritual world, the beings of the spiritual world. We perceive first the images, then the sounds, then the beings and then, finally, the life of these beings. One can only suggest dimly what the pictures of the Imaginative world, as we call it, are like by comparing them symbolically with images drawn from the sense-world. One can only hint at the reality of the 'harmony of the spheres' by comparing it with music on earth. As for the impression we have of beings, at the third stage — that can only be compared with something nowadays known only in the inner-most nature of man, when he feels he is acting in accordance with the divine will. When a person's will is in accordance with the spiritual powers who bring about the progress of the world, his nature will be in a similar condition and he will be able to perceive in this sphere. And whatever is in him which opposes the forward movement of the world or retards its progress, he perceives as something which must be thrown off in this world, something which must fall away like the last veil. Thus the pupil perceives first a world of spiritual images, symbols of a spiritual reality; then a world of cosmic harmonies, symbolically pointing to a higher spiritual sphere; then a world of spiritual beings, comparable in modern experience only with what he finds in the depths of his own being, working with the spiritual powers of good — or evil. The initiand has to pass through these three stages, each of which is reflected faithfully in the Apocalypse of John.

It begins with the physical world: everything pertaining to the physical world or which can be communicated by physical means is said in the Seven Letters. Letters are what we use in the physical world to express our intentions for external cultural life, or to address those working in the physical world. The word, embodied in a letter, can produce an effect in the sense-perceptible world. Thus the first stage furnishes symbols, which have to be correlated with the spiritual reality of what they express.

After the Seven Letters comes the world of the Seven Seals, the world of images — the first stage of initiation.

Then comes the world of cosmic harmonies, perceived by those with spiritual hearing: it is represented by the Seven Trumpets.

The next world, where the initiate perceives beings, is the stage at which beings enter and strip away the shells of the forces opposed to the good. Now the opposite of divine love is divine wrath: the true form of divine love, which moves the world forward upon its path, is perceived in this third sphere by those who have stripped away the seven shells (or husks) of wrath for the physical world.

Thus by stages the initiand ascends through the several spheres of initiation.

The son of man

John turns round, and he sees 'seven golden lights.' And:

> Among the lights was one like a Son of Man, dressed
> in a robe reaching down to his feet and with a golden
> sash round his chest. His head and his hair were white
> like wool, as white as snow, and his eyes were like
> blazing fire.[16]

Subsequently we are told that 'the seven lights are the Seven
Communities.'[17] Hence we must understand them as seven
different ways to the divine, each in itself more or less imperfect. But the Son of Man also 'had in his right hand seven
stars,'[18] and 'the seven stars are the angels of the Seven Communities.'[19] The guiding spirits or *daimons* of mysteriosophy
have here become the guiding angels of the Seven Communities, which are thus presented as the bodies of spiritual entities, of which the angels are the soul on the analogy of the
human soul as the guiding power over the body. Each Community represents a way to the divine from a certain limited
point of view, and the guides along these ways are the angels. They must therefore come to accept as their own leader
the being who in his right hand holds the 'seven stars.'

> And out of his mouth issued a sharp two-edged
> sword, and his countenance resembled the shining sun
> in its glory.[20]

This sword also figures in the Mysteries: the initiand was
terrified by a 'drawn sword.' Such is the situation of one who
wants actual experience of the divine — who wants the
countenance of wisdom to shine upon him like the sun, as
does John: it is a testing of his inner strength.

From: *Das Christentum als mystische Tatsache.*

> And when I saw him, I fell at his feet as if dead. He
> laid his right hand on me and said, 'Do not be
> afraid.'[21]

The experiences which must be undergone by the initiand are
ones otherwise undergone only when someone dies. The one
who guides him through them has to take him into realms
where birth and death no longer have any meaning. The
initiated one therefore enters on a 'new life':

> And I was dead, but see! I am alive throughout all the
> cycles of time. And I hold the keys of Death and the
> underworld.[22]

Thus John is brought to the stage of beholding the Mysteries
of existence.

> And after this I looked, and saw the door of heaven
> open. And the first voice which was heard was like a
> Trumpet sounding and it said to me, 'Ascend to this
> place and I will reveal what must take place
> hereafter.'[23]

The messages which were proclaimed to the Seven Churches
taught John what had to happen in the physical realm in
order to prepare the way for Christianity. What he now sees
'in the spirit' leads him to a vision of the spiritual sources of
reality.

These are things still hidden behind the physical processes,
but after further physical development they will be manifested in a future, spiritualized condition of the world. The
initiate experiences spiritually in the present what will be
realized in the course of time to come:

> And immediately I was in the spirit. And I saw in
> heaven a Throne. And there was one sitting upon
> the Throne, whose appearance was like jasper and

carnelian. And there was a rainbow like emerald
encircling the Throne ... Also before the Throne
was what looked like a sea of glass, clear like
crystal.[24]

The images in which the vision is clothed by the seer depict
the sources or archetypes of perceptible reality.[25]

And in the sphere around the Throne were twenty-
four thrones, upon which were seated the twenty-four
Elders, clad in flowing white and with golden crowns
upon their heads.[26]

Around the archetypal source of reality we thus find beings
who have already advanced far along the path of wisdom,
who look upon the Infinite and bear witness to it.

In the centre and around the Throne were the Four
Living Creatures, full of eyes before and behind. The
first Living Creature was like a lion. The second was
like a bull. The third looked like a man. The fourth
was like a flying eagle. And each of the Four Living
Creatures had six wings and was full of eyes around
and within. And they cry without ceasing, both day
and night, 'Holy, Holy, Holy, is God, the Almighty,
who was, and is, and is to come.'[27]

It is easy to understand the Living Creatures: they represent
the supersensible life which underlies the forms of all living
beings. Later they raise their voices in response to the sound
of the Trumpets — i.e. when the life contained in physical
forms is transformed and spiritualized.

The book with seven seals

The one who sits enthroned holds in his right hand a book, which marks out the path to the summit of wisdom. Only one person is worthy to open this book:

> Look! the Lion of the tribe of Judah, the root of David, has triumphed. He is able to open the book and its seven seals.[28]

The book has seven seals — human wisdom is sevenfold. Once again we encounter the holiness of the number seven.

'Seals,' in the mystical philosophy of Philo Judaeus, are the eternal cosmic Ideas which come to expression in things.[29] Human wisdom is the quest for these creative Ideas. Only in the book sealed by them can divine Wisdom be found. The archetypal Ideas behind the created world must be unveiled — the seals opened — and the contents of the book will be revealed. Jesus is the Lion who can break open the seals: he has given a meaning to the Ideas of creation so as to point the way to Wisdom.

The Lamb that was slain, which God has dearly bought with the price of his own blood, is Jesus who as the bearer of the Christ has passed in the profoundest sense through the Mystery of life and death: it is he who opens the book.[30]

Each time one of the seals is opened, the Living Creatures declare what they know. When the First Seal is broken, John sees a White Horse, on which sits a rider with a bow. The first universal power or embodiment of the Idea of creation becomes visible. It has a new rider, Christianity, who sets it on the right track. And through the new faith, strife is allayed.

With the opening of the Second Seal, a Red Horse appears. Again it has a rider. He takes away Peace — the second of

From: *Das Christentum als mystische Tatsache.*

the universal powers — from the earth so that humanity should not neglect through sloth the cultivation of the spiritual life.

When the Third Seal is opened, the universal power of Justice, now led by Christianity, appears; with the opening of the Fourth, it is the power of Religion which appears and which is given a new perspective through Christianity. The significance of the Four Living Creatures emerges clearly: they are the four chief universal powers which are to be given a new direction by Christianity.[31]

War	Lion
Peaceful work	Bull
Justice	Human countenance
Religious aspiration	Eagle

The meaning of the third Being is made explicit when the Third Seal is opened and the text reads:

> A quart of wheat for a day's wages, three quarts of barley for a day's wages.

Thus the rider carries a pair of scales. When the Fourth Seal is opened, the rider who appears is called 'Death, and Hell was following close behind him': the rider stands for righteousness in Religion.[32]

When the Fifth Seal is opened, the souls of those who have already taken up Christianity appear: the creative Idea behind Christianity itself is manifested. But this refers only to the first stage of Christian society, which is no less transitory than the other manifestations of the creative Ideas.

The Sixth Seal is opened. And now it is revealed that the spiritual world of Christianity is something eternal. The people are pervaded by the spiritual reality which actually brought Christianity into existence. They are themselves made holy by what they have created:

> And I heard the number of those who were sealed:
> one hundred and forty-four thousand out of all the
> tribes of the children of Israel were sealed.[33]

These are the ones who prepared the way for the Eternal
before it took the form of Christianity, and who have been
transformed by the impetus given through Christ.

Then comes the opening of the Seventh Seal. This reveals
what true Christianity ought really to be for the world. The
seven angels 'who stand before God' appear. These angels
are once again spiritual Beings known in the ancient Mysteries translated into Christian terms. They stand for the true
Christian path to the divine vision. The next stage is thus a
leading into the presence of God. It is an initiation which
John will undergo.

The seven trumpets

I

The proclamations of the angels are accompanied by the
necessary features of all initiation. When the first angel blew
upon his Trumpet:

> There followed hail and fire mingled with blood, and
> it was hurled down upon the earth. A third part of the
> earth was burned up, together with a third part of the
> trees, and all of the green grass.[34]

Similar portents occur when the other angels blow upon their
Trumpets.

However, we also notice that this is not simply an initiation of the kind known in ancient times, but a new form
of initiation which is to replace the old. Unlike the ancient

From: *Das Christentum als mystische Tatsache.*

Mysteries, Christianity does not exist only for the sake of a few chosen individuals: it is addressed to all humanity, and aspires to be the religion of all people. The truth of Christianity is accessible to everyone who 'has ears to hear.' The *mystai* of the ancient world were singled out from the multitude; but the Christian Trumpets sound for all who are willing to hear them. How to respond is a matter for every one to decide. That is the reason why the terrors in this 'initiation of all humanity' are also so enormously enhanced.

Through his initiation, John sees the condition of the earth and its inhabitants in the far future. The underlying idea behind this is that the seer in the higher worlds already beholds what still lies in the future for the world below. The Seven Letters present the meaning of Christianity for the present age; the Seven Seals show what is being prepared now for the future through Christianity.[35] The future remains as yet veiled, under seal, for the uninitiated. In the process of initiation the seals are opened. At the end of the time covered by the Seven Letters, the earthly age begins to pass over into a more spiritual condition. Life will no longer be limited as it is in its present physical forms, but will appear even externally as an imaging of the supersensible archetypes — represented by the Four Living Creatures and the other pictures connected with the Seals. Still further ahead in the future the earth will take on the form intimated to the initiates by the sounding of the Trumpets.

In this way the initiate has a 'prophetic' experience of future conditions. The initiate into the Christian Mystery experiences the impetus given to life on earth by the entering and onward working of the Christ. Meanwhile everything which remains bound up with the transitory and falls short of true Christianity is shown as meeting death. Then a powerful angel appears, with a little book open in his hand which he gives to John:

> He said to me, 'Take it and eat it. It will be bitter
> in your stomach, but sweet like honey in your
> mouth.'[36]

John is instructed not just to peruse the little book, but to absorb it completely, to make its contents part of himself. Of what value is knowledge if it is not a living power in man's life? Wisdom must be such a living power. The goal is not mere knowledge of the divine: it is the divinization of man. But knowledge of the kind contained in the little book is painful to the transitory nature in man, and is 'bitter in the stomach.' To the same extent however it is bliss to his eternal nature and so 'sweet in the mouth like honey.'

If Christianity is to become a real force upon earth it can only be in this way — through an initiation of humanity. Thus it strikes dead all that still belongs to man's lower nature:

> Their corpses will lie in the street of the great City,
> which spiritually is called Sodom and Egypt, where
> their Lord was also crucified.[37]

By these are meant the adherents of Christ, who will be persecuted by the powers of this transitory world. However, it is only in their own transitory nature that they suffer and for their true self it is an inner victory. Their destiny mirrors the archetypal destiny which was that of Christ Jesus. The 'City, which spiritually is called Sodom and Egypt' is the symbol for the life which remains confined to externals and does not take into itself the transforming impetus of the Christ. Christ is crucified everywhere in the lower nature. Where the lower nature triumphs, everything remains dead: the streets of the City are strewn with corpses. But those who overcome their lower nature and awaken the crucified Christ to new life hear the proclamation of the angel with the Seventh Trumpet:

The kingdoms of the world have become those of the
Lord and of his Anointed, who will reign from
eternity to eternity.[38]

Upon which 'the Temple of God in heaven was opened, and
the ark of his covenant became visible there.'[39]

II

The Apocalyptist presents things which are actually experienced by anyone who makes the ascent into the realms of the
spiritual world. He shows us things transcending the earthly.
He shows us the moment in the future when earthly substance will be liberated from matter and dissolve into the
spiritual.

Two forces also appear which point to the connection of
the earth with the cosmos in the evolutionary past: Wisdom
and Power. With them appears the force which indicates
fulfilment for the mission of earthly life — namely, Love
which is unfolded by humanity.* The whole then appears to
us as a personification of the man of the future. The future
form of humanity confronts us here in this symbolic vision,
supported by the forces of Wisdom and Power, pervaded by
Love. The book which he has before him, the Gospel of Love,
is a book which does not just work from outside but which
has to be consumed. Hence arises the tremendous image that
meets us in this passage:

And I beheld another powerful angel who came down
out of heaven. He was wrapped in a cloud as his
garment, with a rainbow over his head. His
countenance was like the sun, and his feet were like

From *Die Apokalypse des Johannes,* extract from lecture 8.

* We have represented this in a symbolic way in our Fourth Seal. The
forms appear reversed because they indicate something which has not yet
happened.

pillars of fire. He was holding in his hand a little book
lying open, and he set his right foot upon the sea and
his left foot upon the land.[40]

'I saw another powerful angel': the being has to be represented as such because it stands far above the level of
present-day humanity. 'Who came down out of spiritual
spheres' — that is how it appears to the seer — 'who was
wrapped in a cloud as his garment ... his countenance was
like the sun, and his feet like pillars, like pillars of fire': these
are the two forces already referred to, which come to the
earth as a heritage from the cosmos. 'And he had in his hand
a little book lying open, and he set his right foot upon the
sea and his left foot upon the land.' Then John asks the angel
to give him the little book:

> He said to me, 'Take it and eat it. It will be bitter in
> your stomach, but sweet like honey in your mouth ...'
> And I took the little book from the angel's hand and
> ate it, and it was sweet like honey in my mouth ... [41]

That is how the seer's experience has to be described. His
gaze has reached the point where the earth will pass over
from the physical and material state into a spiritual or 'astral'
one. At that point the mission of the earth will be completed.
And it is then that the seer learns the real import of the
Gospel of Love, the impetus given to human development in
the fourth age,[42] so that like the Apocalyptist he experiences
blessedness, already in this life. He knows already the state
of bliss prepared for humanity. And yet he experiences it in
the present-day body — for however high the being which
would take on life with humanity, it must be embodied in
flesh. And although in many ways the present-day condition
of the body offers the spirit the possibility of developing to
a high level, by the very same token it brings the possibility
of intense suffering. Therefore the soul of the Apocalyptist is
able to ascend, as he has described, into spiritual regions and

there receive the Gospel of Love, experiencing the spiritual bliss which is 'sweet like honey in the mouth.' But because he lives in the present-day body he has to admit that the ascent produces in many respects the reverse of bliss — that is what he means by saying that the little book at first tastes sweet like honey, but gives him severe pain in the stomach. And that is only a small reflection of what it means 'to be crucified in the body,' which is the symbolic expression for the fact that the higher the spirit ascends, the harder it becomes for it to dwell in the body.

666: the Beast and the abyss

I

The initiate's experience brings back in a new form the primaeval struggle between the higher and lower natures. On the Christian path, everything that the initiates in the older Mysteries had to undergo must be recapitulated. As Osiris was threatened by the evil Typhon, so now there is 'the great Dragon, the ancient Snake' to be defeated.

The Woman (the human soul) gives birth to the lower knowledge, but unless this is intensified to the point of becoming wisdom it remains an adverse power. It is a stage to be passed through. In the Apocalypse this lower knowledge appears in the guise of 'the ancient Snake':

> A great and wonderful sign appeared in heaven: a
> Woman clothed with the Sun, with the Moon under
> her feet and a crown of twelve stars on her head. She
> was with child and cried out for she was about to give
> birth. And another sign appeared in heaven: an
> enormous red Dragon with seven heads and ten horns
> and seven crowns on his heads ... [43]

From: *Das Christentum als mystische Tatsache.*

From far back the wisdom of the *mystai* had used the snake as its symbol of knowledge. The Snake — knowledge — may be a seductive force, however, unless man brings to life within himself the 'Son of God.'[44] He it is who crushes the serpent's head:

> The great Dragon was hurled down — that ancient
> Snake who is called the Devil and Satan and seduces
> all the world — he was hurled down upon the earth,
> together with his angels.[45]

The passage shows Christianity's intention to become a renewed form of initiation: to achieve in a new way what was done in the Mysteries. For they too were intended to overcome the power of the Snake, although there were to be differences from the former ways of proceeding.

II

The Christ-being is represented as the spirit of the Sun, who has united himself with the earth and so become the spirit of the earth, from the time of the Mystery of Golgotha onward.

But there is also a principle opposed to the Lamb: a Sun-Demon who is active in man's evil doings and pushes back the influence of the Lamb. Hence a certain part of the human race is thrust out from the path of development which would unite it with the Sun. These forces stand in opposition to the Sun, as negative Sun-forces. When 666 cosmic stages have passed, they will have the tendency to be cast out altogether from the path of human development. They will ultimately be cast into the abyss. Thus we must distinguish not only the Beast with seven heads and ten horns, as he is symbolically represented, but also the Beast provided with forces which oppose the Sun. At the stage when the earth is to be united

From *Die Apokalypse des Johannes*, extract from lecture 11.

with the Sun, when the 666 stages are fulfilled, these are destined to disappear into the abyss.

Now this number 666 has always been written down in a very mysterious way. (Later we shall see that there is every reason for the facts we are now discussing to be shrouded in mystery. Hence it is veiled and only written out as 666.) The Apocalyptist had received his initiation in Mysteries where it was written: 400 + 200 + 6 + 60. This is unintelligible to the ordinary person. 666 remains a mystery, a blind which conceals behind it 400 + 200 + 6 + 60. But the way of writing used by the initiates was based on the principle that letters may stand for the numbers which correspond to them. This was used to interpret the number 666 by a series of noteworthy exegetes in the nineteenth century, but of their efforts one might say that although they hit a number of bells they did not manage to ring the chimes. They were not very clear about the esoteric teaching which I have just described, and when they discovered that by using the values of the Hebrew alphabet, 'Nero' adds up to 666, they concluded that the number was supposed to signify Nero — a wrong conclusion.[46] The meaning can be reached only by first writing 400 + 200 + 6 + 60.

Then one must write 400 as ת (tau), 200 as ר (resh), 6 as ו (vau) and 60 as ס (samekh). These are the corresponding Hebrew letters and with wonderful ingenuity they have been drawn into this mystery because of the special, hidden significance which attaches to these four sounds. Consider what the number 666 must actually mean in view of the explanation given above: it means the principle which leads to the utter hardening of man in external matters, forcing him to reject what would enable him to shrug off the lower attributes and rise above them to higher things. The four lower principles — physical, etheric and astral bodies together with the lower self, before it begins to transform itself into the higher self — are represented by these four letters. Thus the four letters collectively express the state of being hardened in the four lower principles, before they begin their process of 'divinization.' The Apocalyptist can truly say that here is wisdom. Wisdom is indeed concealed within them:

> Whoever has understanding, let him calculate the number of the Beast ... His number is 666.

We are now in a position to read the name. We must read it, of course, from right to left and we must add the vowels. Then we read: סורת, Sorat.

Sorat is the name of the Sun-Demon, the enemy of the Lamb. Each spiritual being was characterized, furthermore, by a sign in addition to a name. The symbol designating

Sorat was: **ﻝ**   — a thick stroke bent back on itself and

terminating in two curved points.[47] Here once again we have to understand what the Apocalyptist really means when, at the outset of the Apocalypse, he uses a striking term which is not in general correctly translated. He says it is 'communicated in signs.' We must take this seriously: the real content of the Mystery is given 'in signs.' For it is actually 'signs' which express the 666 and which he describes in the following terms:

> I beheld another Beast arise, out of the earth. He had two horns like a Lamb.[48]

This is nothing other than the 'sign' with the two curved points on the top, deliberately veiled here because he terms them 'horns.' It was always the practice in the Mysteries to employ ambiguous terms, so as to prevent the uninitiated from gaining easy access to their meaning. But he describes here the sign of the Sun-Demon, known in the Mysteries under the name Sorat — the name whose letters give the numerical value of 666 (400 + 200 + 6 + 60) in an extremely recondite fashion.

The Apocalyptist points, then, to the enemy of the Lamb.

At the juncture when the earth passes over into a spiritual existence, down below the forms of men revert to their animal shapes: the Beast with seven heads and ten horns appears. But there also appears the one who leads astray, the one who has the power to prevent them returning to the Sun, the one who is the enemy of the Christ.

Human beings themselves cannot be enemies of Christ. At most they can fail to seize the opportunity of taking the principle of Christ into themselves because of the power of deception which is in them. But there is an enemy of Christ, and that is the Sun-Demon.

He appears at the instant there is something which can become his prey. Before his prey — the men with the seven heads and ten horns — are there, there is nothing for the tempter to lead astray and he has nothing to seek. But when men appear with the inclinations, then comes the tempter, and then appears the second Beast and leads them astray. Thus at the moment when the earth passes into an astral condition there appears in human nature what existed in him when the earth was still wrapped in water: the human animal appears. From the water rises the Beast with seven heads and ten horns. And because this Beast has had no part in earthly evolution, it is possible for the opponent of the Sun, Sorat, to rise out of the earth.[49] It is this which enables him to approach man and to drag him down with all his might into the abyss.

From this point onward, then, we see clinging to man a being possessed of terrifying power. And what does it do, this being, in order to lead people to the most appalling deeds imaginable? For it is not just a matter of immorality in the ordinary sense — that needs no monster in the shape of the Demon of the Sun. The Beast represented with the two horns only gains power over humanity when the qualities which distinguish the spirits of man's redemption, the qualities which exalt us spiritually, are distorted into their opposite; when things go so far that spirituality is made to serve the interests of the lower self. The ability of the Beast with the two horns to lead us astray is connected with the abuse of spiritual forces.

The misuse of spiritual forces is what we call 'black' magic, as opposed to their proper use in 'white' magic. And the result is that there will be a split in the ranks of humankind, leading on the one hand to increasing spiritualization and the use of spiritual forces in 'white' magic, and on the other to their abuse and to the rampant power of the two-horned Beast, 'black' magic. In the end humanity will be polarized into those who perform 'white' magic and those who perform 'black' magic. Within the mystery of 666 is concealed the further mystery of 'black' magic: the most appalling crime in the whole unfolding of the earth's development. No other crime can be compared with it. The one who leads us astray into 'black' magic is imaged by the Apocalyptist in the two-horned Beast.

Thus there appears on our horizon, in the far future, a polarization of mankind into the 'elect of Christ,' the 'white' magicians, and the savage 'black' magicians, their opponents. The latter cannot extricate themselves from matter. In the language of the Apocalyptist, they 'prostitute' themselves with matter. In his spiritual vision the union between man and the hardening forces in matter takes on the appearance of Babylon: the whole community of 'black' magicians is involved in the unholy marriage or prostitution between man and the disintegrating forces in matter. In the distant future these two powers will confront each other — those who throng the great Babylon, and those who have transcended matter to unite their human nature with the principle of the Lamb.[50] The ones most given to 'black' magic are set apart in 'Babylon' with all the powers opposed to the Sun, led by Sorat the two-horned Beast. On the other hand, from the 'elect' come those who unite themselves with Christ, the Lamb, who manifests himself to them. There is the marriage of the Lamb, and over against it Babylon in the throes of dissolution, sinking into the abyss.

The Mystery-temple

The Christian Mystery was to replace the many Mysteries of the ancient world with its unique, archetypal Mystery-event. In Jesus the *Logos* had become flesh, and he was to become the teacher of initiation to all mankind. His community of *mystai* was to be the human race. In place of the old principle of selecting individuals, there was to be the gathering together of all. Hence everyone was enabled to become a *mystes*, in so far as he was sufficiently mature to do so. The Gospel is proclaimed to all, and whoever has an ear to hear is eager to fathom its mysteries; the heart of each has the decisive voice.

Thus it was no longer a case of introducing one person or another into the temples of the Mysteries, but of the word spoken to all and heard now with more, now with less clarity and strength. And it will be left to the *daimon*, the angel in a person's own breast, to decide how far his initiation can proceed. The Mystery-temple is the entire world:

> I saw the Holy City, the new Jerusalem, coming down
> out of heaven from God, prepared as a Bride
> beautifully dressed for her husband. And I heard a
> loud voice from the Throne saying, 'Now the dwelling
> of God is with men and he will dwell among them.
> They will be his people, and God himself will be with
> them and be their God.'[51]

No longer is blessedness reserved for those who have witnessed within the confines of the Mystery-temples those awe-inspiring enactments which are the types and symbols of eternity. For now 'Blessed are those who have not seen, but who have believed.'[52] Even if at first they wander in

From: *Das Christentum als mystische Tatsache*.

darkness, the light may yet reach them. There is no secrecy; the way opens out for all.

There is much more in the Apocalypse, concerning the threat to Christianity from anti-Christian powers, and the eventual triumph of Christianity. All other gods are taken up into the higher unity of the Christian divinity:

> I did not see a temple in the City, because the Lord, the all-ruling God, and the Lamb are its temple. The City had no need of the Sun nor of the moon to shine upon it, because the revelation of the divine presence is its light, and its lamp is the Lamb.[53]

The Mystery at the heart of the 'Revelation of Saint John' is precisely this: the Mysteries are no longer secret. The angel says to him:

> Do not seal up the prophecies in this book, for the time of God's manifestation is near.[54]

Thus the writer of the Apocalypse expounds, from the standpoint of his own belief, the relationship of his community to those of previous times. His view of the Mysteries has become the content of a Mystery-text. The traditions that have come down about it are appropriate to its Mystery character: the author wrote it down on the island of Patmos, and the revelation is said to have been received in a 'cave.'

Christianity arose out of the Mysteries. In the Apocalypse, Christian wisdom was a Mystery reborn — but a Mystery which breaks out of the framework of the ancient Mysteries. The Mystery of a unique, single event was to become the Mystery with a significance for all.

*   *   *

There is an apparent contradiction in saying that the secrets of the Mysteries became manifest in Christianity but that in the spiritual visions of the Apocalyptist we nevertheless observe a 'Christian Mystery.'

To solve the enigma, we must reflect how it was that the secrets of the ancient Mysteries were revealed. It was through the historical events in Palestine, which drew back the veil from what had previously been kept hidden in the Mysteries. Something was introduced into the history of the world through the appearance of Christ, and it is this which constitutes the new Mystery. The initiates of former ages had seen in the spirit how events were leading towards the manifestation of the 'hidden' Christ; but with the Christian initiate it is a matter of the 'hidden' effects which spring from the Christ who now has been 'revealed.'

7. The Rediscovery of the Cosmic Christ

It is perhaps a paradox that the thrust of Steiner's underlying argument, namely that in Christianity the Mysteries assumed the form required by the evolving individuality of man, should lead to the rediscovery in the twentieth century of the cosmic Christ. The prehistoric Mystery-cults had taken the individual out of the familiar, everyday world in order to communicate the cosmic meaning of life. Christianity had turned the Mysteries into a force that could lead individuals to grow and develop spiritually while still engaging with the world, while still actively shaping their society as active members. It was one of the greatest of early Christianity's tragedies that the new emphasis came to be understood in an exclusive way, as implying a denial of humanity's cosmic role. And yet, in the way Steiner tackles the problems of mankind's evolution, we may understand why this was necessary. Rather as we cannot in practice give teenagers the sensible conclusions drawn from our own life-experience, so with a step-forward in human evolution there cannot be a simple handing on of the old alongside the new. What is important, however, is that now we can indeed begin to rediscover the full potential of Christianity for the individual and society in transformation. And as modern individuals, the Mystery-process will lead us to the understanding of the cosmic Christ which the historical Church largely forgot. Reaching back behind the rigid formulations of later dogma, Steiner recreates the original idea of the Trinity as stages of God's revelation to humanity, the 'plan of salvation' — only later did it become a speculation on

From: *Nordische und mitteleuropäische Geist-impulse. Das Fest der Erscheinung Christi.* Extract from a lecture given in Basle, December 26, 1921 (GA no. 209).

the inner workings of God's being. And he places the Christmas festival of the earthly appearance of Jesus once more in relation to the cosmic festival, the new Christmas which we can experience again as a result. While not forgetting the way Christianity brought spiritual values to multitudes of people, he restores to it the higher goal of a human and individual response to a cosmic revelation.

Thus when it instituted the Christmas festival in the fourth century, Christianity was contributing towards a union of people all over the earth. For connected with the festival of Christmas was something of a dearly loved and cherished nature: only consider how over the centuries we have proof from all sides that as Christmas drew near, the soul of every Christian was filled with devoted love for the infant Jesus. And behind that devoted love lies something of tremendous significance for all the centuries which came afterwards. We must strive to understand too what it meant that the festival of Christmas was fixed on December 25 — which is to say, more or less at the winter solstice. For actually as late as AD 353, even in Rome, the festival was not celebrated on December 25. Nor, for that matter, was it a celebration of the birth of Jesus of Nazareth.

The festival was celebrated on January 6, and commemorated the baptism in the Jordan. It commemorated the Christ-being, and was focussed upon the idea that at the baptism in the Jordan a being who belonged to a world transcending the earthly world, the Christ, had descended from the heavens and become one with human nature in the person of Jesus of Nazareth.[1] The birth that it celebrated was not an ordinary birth. The festival celebrated the descent of the Christ-being, through which new forces, forces of renewal, poured into earthly life; it was the Christ-epiphany, remembered as the Mystery of a heavenly power uniting with the earth. And through the intervention of heaven, human development had received a new impetus.[2] At the time of the Event on Golgotha, and for a short period afterwards, this mystery of a heavenly being who descended into earthly existence was still understood. In a fragmentary form there still remained the archaic wisdom capable of grasping truths from supersensory experience. The ancient knowledge, instinctive in nature, had flowed into earth-born humanity as a gift of the gods — but this ancient wisdom was gradually lost, fading gradually away over the centuries. Yet at the time of the Mystery of Golgotha, humanity still possessed that wisdom in sufficient measure to comprehend the magnitude of what had come about. And so in the early centuries of Christianity, it was by wisdom that the Mystery of Golgotha was understood.[3]

But by the fourth century AD, this wisdom had almost completely faded away. Humanity's attention was seized rather by the pagan peoples, flooding in from all directions.[4] Understanding of the deep mystery of the joining of Christ to the man Jesus was no longer possible. The real meaning of the Mystery of Golgotha was lost to the human soul, and remained so throughout the centuries that followed. The ancient wisdom was lost to humanity — and necessarily so, since on the basis of this wisdom man could never have achieved his condition of autonomy, of freedom. It was necessary that humanity enter for a while into the darkness, in order that it should be able to unfold, out of the darkness, out of freedom, its own authentic powers.

By a genuinely Christian instinct, however, another quality was put forward in place of the wisdom with which the early Christian world had interpreted the Mystery of Golgotha, and which brought light to the discussions about the nature of the Mystery that took place among the wise Fathers of the Church — another and quite different quality. Yet modern Christianity has little comprehension of the profundity of those discussions in the early centuries of Christianity concerning the 'union of the two natures,' divine and human, in the personality of Jesus of Nazareth.[5] To the early Christian centuries it was a mystery that called upon a vital wisdom, which afterwards faded into empty abstractions. In Western

Christianity, very little has remained of the holy passion with which men struggled to grasp how, in the Mystery of Golgotha, human and divine had been joined in one. But the impulse of Christianity is great and powerful. It was the power of love which came to replace the wisdom that had been there to greet the Mystery of Golgotha, its radiance still shining out over the earth.[6]

Throughout the centuries, in marvellous abundance, love for the infant Jesus lying in the manger has poured out of the hearts and minds of humanity.* But if we let these things affect us we shall become aware how deeply the Christmas festival is a festival of retrospection. The wisdom of the people from Old Testament times had as its aim that they should return and be gathered to the bosom of their fathers; similarly the people of New Testament times have striven to gather together at Christmas, to look back with devoted love on the innocent child lying in the manger.† The people of Old Testament times yearned to return to their origin — their fathers, the ancestors. And a Christian is turning his mind and heart to the original purity of human nature when he celebrates the birth of Jesus. The same Christian instinct which made people associate the Christmas festival with their earthly origins also prompted the dedication of the previous day, December 24, to Adam and Eve. The day of Adam and Eve fell before the day of the birth of Jesus, and out of the same instinct the Tree of Paradise came by association to be the symbol of Christmas. First of all we contemplate the infant lying in the manger at Bethlehem, with the animals grouped around the holy Mother: it is a heavenly symbol of the origins of humanity. Our feelings and

* It is wonderful, too, to find how strongly that love is reflected in the nativity plays which have come down to us from the earlier centuries of Christianity![7]

† But who will deny that the pouring-out of love to the well-spring of Christianity from all those hearts has in time become little more than a habit? Who will deny that the Christmas festival has gradually lost its vitality?

thoughts are carried back to the origins of mankind on earth, to the Tree of Paradise. The crib is associated with this Tree of Paradise, just as in the *Golden Legend* the earthly origins of mankind are associated with the Mystery of Golgotha. In the *Golden Legend* the wood of the Tree of Paradise is said to have come down in a miraculous way from generation to generation until the epoch of the Mystery of Golgotha. The cross erected on Golgotha, the 'place of the skull,' the cross on which Jesus hung, was made of the very same wood of the Tree of Paradise![8] In other words, the heavenly origin of man was mixed up with his earthly origin.

In another sense, too, a basic Christian conception has only tended to blur the issue here. Nobody can fail to observe that there is little understanding nowadays for what is yet the truth concerning the Godhead which can be venerated as the Father, or first-principle, but can also be conceived as the 'Son.' People in general, and equally our supposedly enlightened theology, have lost sight of the distinction in nature between God the Father and God the Son. Any insight into it has been lost. Indeed, according to the standard teachings of modern theology in their latest form, the Gospels point to God the Father — but not to God the Son. Jesus of Nazareth is to be regarded as a great teacher, whose message concerned the Father God.

When people speak of Christ today, his name still bears with it certain associations carried over from sacred scripture, but they have no clearly defined sense of the distinction in nature between God the Son and God the Father. But that sense was still very much alive at the period when the Mystery of Golgotha was fulfilled in earthly actuality. In part of the Near East, a region of no special significance to Rome at that time, the Christ had appeared in Jesus of Nazareth. According to the primitive Christians, Christ was that divine Being who had ensouled a human being in a way without parallel before or after; and this unique Event of Golgotha, or ensouling of a human being by a divine Being, the Christ, gives its meaning to the whole development of the earth. All previous development comes to be seen as a preparation, and all subsequent development the fulfilment, the unfolding of the Mystery of Golgotha.[9]

Now this Event took place in the Near East while on the imperial throne in Rome sat Augustus Caesar. People nowadays do not always grasp that Augustus Caesar in Rome was regarded as the embodiment of deity — that the Caesars were actually held to be gods in human form. Here then we have two totally alien conceptions of a God! The one a God on the throne in Rome, the other on Golgotha, the 'place of the skull.' No greater contrast is possible![10] Just consider the fact that Augustus was regarded as a divinity embodied in a human being. In him a divine being was thought to have descended to earth, and united with the forces of generation, of blood-descent. A divinity had penetrated into earthly existence and was present in the pulsation of the blood. Some such idea, in various forms, was prevalent throughout the ancient world, according to which the Godhead dwelled on earth, being bound up with the forces of the blood.* People said, *Ex Deo nascimur:* Out of God we are born. Even people of the lower ranks felt that they had a relationship to what lived as the crown of human society in one such as Augustus Caesar. And what was thus honoured and worshipped was the divine Father-principle — a principle living in the blood of a human being when he was born into the world.

What had happened in the Mystery of Golgotha, however, was that the divine Christ-being had united himself to the man Jesus of Nazareth, not with the blood but with the highest forces of the soul of man. In this case a God had joined himself to a human being in such a way that mankind was rescued from falling victim to the earthly forces of matter. God the Father is a living presence in the blood; the Son lives in the soul and spirit of man. The Father leads man

---

* It is among the Jews alone that we find the experience of a God utterly transcending the world.

over into material existence — Out of God we are born; God
the Son leads man out of material existence once more. God
the Father leads humanity from the supersensible into the
material world; God the Son, out of the material and into the
supersensible. *In Christo morimur:* In Christ we die. Two
totally different feelings are involved. To the feeling connected with God the Father was added the feeling, the
perception of God the Son.

Certain driving forces in man's process of development
have brought it about, however, that the faculty of distinguishing between God the Father and the Son was lost. They
continue to be present, both among mankind generally and
within Christianity, to the present day. The people who once
possessed the archaic wisdom of primaeval times knew, from
their own inner experiences, that they had descended from
divine-spiritual worlds into physical, material life. Pre-
existence was a fact universally certain and accepted. People
looked back through birth, through conception, to the divine-
spiritual worlds above from which at birth the soul descends
into physical existence.[11] But in our language we have only
the word for not-dying, 'immortality': we have no expression
for the other side of eternity, no such word as 'innatality'!
And yet if our conception of eternity is to be complete, the
term for unbornness must be there to complement immortality. Indeed the potential significance of 'unbornness' is even
greater than that of immortality.

True it is that the human being passes through the gate of
death into life in the spiritual world. But it is no less true that
the notion of this life which people are presented with
nowadays is an extremely egotistical one. Living here on
earth, human beings long for immortality; they do not want
to subside into nothingness at death. Hence when speaking
of immortality, it is only necessary to appeal to men's
instinctive selfishness. Listen carefully to any number of
sermons, and they will be found to base themselves upon
the self-centredness of human beings when trying to convey
the idea of immortality to their souls. With the conception

of 'unbornness,' however, it is impossible to base oneself on such impulses. People do not have the egotistical
interest in existing before birth in the spiritual world which
they have in ensuring a life in the spiritual world after
death. It is enough that a place in the hereafter is assured for
them; why should they trouble about whence they have
come?

Out of egotism men wish to know about a hereafter; but
when a wisdom untainted with self-seeking emerges once
again, unbornness will be as significant as immortality is at
present. In ancient times people were aware that they had
lived in divine-spiritual worlds, and descended through birth
into material form. They felt that the forces which surrounded them in a purely spiritual environment lived on,
united with the blood. From that insight arose the idea 'Out
of God we are born.' The God who lives on in the blood, the
God whom the fleshly man on earth represents, is God the
Father. But the other pole of life, namely death, demands a
different dynamic in the life of the soul. There must be
something in the human being which is not exhausted with
death. Corresponding to this is the conception of the God
who leads the earthly and physical over into the supersensible, the super-physical: the God connected with the Mystery
of Golgotha. Quite correctly, the divine Father-principle has
always been associated with the transition from the supersensible into the material world; through God the Son comes the
transition from the perceptible and material into the spiritual.
That is why the idea of resurrection is intrinsically bound up
with the Mystery of Golgotha. Paul's words, that Christ is
what he is for humanity in virtue of his being the Risen One,
are crucial to the whole conception of Christianity.[12] Only in
the course of the centuries has understanding of the Risen
One, the one who overcame death, gradually been lost until
modern theology concerns itself wholly with the man Jesus
of Nazareth. But a human being, Jesus of Nazareth, cannot be
placed alongside God the Father as a principle on the same
level. He might be regarded as the proclaimer of the Father,

but he could not be placed alongside the Father God as the early Christians asserted.

They came to regard as strictly equal the divine Father and the divine Son. The Father brings about the transition from the supersensible to the material: *Ex Deo nascimur;* Out of God we are born. The Son brings about the transition from the material to the supersensible: *In Christo morimur;* In Christ we die. And transcending birth and death there is the third divine principle, proceeding from and coeval with the Father and the Son, namely the Holy Spirit. In man's own being we see a transition from the supersensible into the material state, and then from the material into the supersensible. The principle which knows neither birth nor death is the Spirit into which and through which we are awakened to new life. *Per Spiritum Sanctum reviviscimus:* Through the Holy Spirit we shall be awakened to new life.[13] For many centuries Christmas has been a festival of remembrance. The extent to which the actual substance of the festival has been lost is amply shown by the fact that of the being Christ Jesus all that remains is the man, Jesus of Nazareth. But for us today Christmas must become a call and a summons to something new.

A new reality must be born. Christianity today needs an impetus of renewal. In so far as it no longer understands the Christ-being in Jesus of Nazareth, Christianity has lost its meaning and direction. The meaning, the essence of Christianity, has to be discovered again, and humanity must learn to realize that the meaning of the Mystery of Golgotha can only be grasped through a knowledge of the supersensible. For another factor, too, stands in the way of understanding the Mystery of Golgotha. Just as we can gaze lovingly on the infant in the manger but lack the intuitive knowledge concerning the union of Christ with the man Jesus of Nazareth, so neither can we look up to heaven's heights with the same intensity of emotion as was the case with the men who lived at the time of the Mystery of Golgotha. In those days people looked up to the world of stars, and in their

orbits and constellations they saw something like the 'countenance' belonging to the divine soul or spirit of the universe.
They could see the Christ-being, as the spiritual principle of
the cosmos, visibly expressed in the splendours of the starry
worlds.[14] But for modern man the worlds of stars, all the
realms of cosmic space, have become little more than a
product of calculation, of celestial mechanics.

The universe has been emptied of the gods. Out of this
cosmos which is devoid of gods, the world investigated by
modern-day physics and astronomy, the Christ-being could
never have descended. In the light of the archaic wisdom
once possessed by humanity, this universe was altogether
different. It was the body of the divine world-soul and the
divine world-spirit, and from this spiritual cosmos the Christ
descended to earth and united with a human being, Jesus of
Nazareth. What really happened is embodied in history itself
in a profound way. For in the time before the Mystery of
Golgotha, all over the earth there were Mysteries — sacred
sites that were centres of learning but at the same time
schools for the cultivation of religious life. And in them were
given indications about what must take place in the future.
It was revealed in the Mysteries that man carries within his
own nature a power that is the conqueror of death. The
victory over death was an actual experience of the initiates in
the Mysteries. From deep experience, the candidate for
initiation acquired the sure conviction of having awakened
within himself the power which overcomes death. In image-
form, the neophyte experienced a process whose full reality
would only unfold in times to come, in accordance with the
grand design of world-history. But in the Mysteries of all the
peoples, this sacred truth was proclaimed: Man can be
victorious over death.

It was also indicated that what could now be presented
only in images in the Mysteries would one day become a real
event, a unique happening in the history of the world. The
Mystery of Golgotha was proclaimed in advance by the
pagan Mysteries in the ancient world. It was the fulfilment

of what had everywhere been heralded in the temples and holy places of the Mysteries.[15]

After due preparation in the Mysteries, consisting of an arduous training that led him to the point of initiation, when he had made his soul so free of the body that it could fuse with and perceive the spiritual worlds, and when he was convinced through experience that in human nature life ultimately triumphs over death, the neophyte then confronted the profoundest experience of all which these ancient Mysteries contained. That was, that the obstacle of earth itself, the obstacle of matter which blots out the reality which is both spiritual and material at once, namely the sun, had to be removed. The candidate was brought to experience a mysterious phenomenon indeed, though it is one well known to every initiate. He 'beheld the sun at midnight' — saw the sun through the earth, at the other side of the earth![16]

An instinctive feeling for the most holy and sacred things has actually persisted, in spite of everything, throughout history. The feeling or perception may have weakened, but to an unprejudiced eye the archaic meaning is still discernible. Hence we may draw conclusions from the fact that at midnight between December 24 and 25, a midnight eucharist is supposed to be held in every Christian church. We can draw our conclusions from this fact if we realize that the eucharist (the Mass) is nothing more nor less than a synthesis of the cultic rites of the Mysteries which led to initiation — to beholding the 'sun at midnight.'[17] The institution of the midnight eucharist at Christmas is an echo of the initiation-rites which permitted the neophyte at the midnight hour to behold the sun at the other side of the earth, and therewith to behold the universe as a spiritual universe. For at the same instant, the cosmic Word resounded through the universe — the cosmic Word, which from the orbits and constellations of the stars intoned the Mysteries of universal Being.

Blood sets human beings in opposition to one another. Blood fetters to the earthly and material that element in humanity which has come down out of heavenly heights. In our own century above all, people have sinned against the essence of Christianity by turning back to the blood-principle. What they must do is find the way to that being, who was Christ Jesus and does not address himself to the blood — rather he poured out his blood and gave it to the earth — who speaks to the soul and the spirit, who unites, not separates, so that peace may arise on earth among men out of their understanding of the cosmic Word.[18]

With a new understanding of the Christmas festival, supersensible knowledge can transform the material universe into a spiritual one before the eye of the soul. It can so transform it that the sun becomes visible at midnight and is known in its spiritual nature. Such knowledge brings us to understand the Christ-being in his nature, which transcends the earthly, as the Sun-being who was once united with Jesus of Nazareth. It should bring us to understand, too, the nature of that peace which should hover over and make as one all the peoples of the earth.

'Divine beings are revealed in the heights; and through this revelation, peace rings out from the hearts of men who are of good will.' It is the word proclaimed at Christmas. Peace on earth flows into and merges with the divine Light that streams down upon the earth. We need more than a remembering of the day on which Jesus was born; we must realize the need for a new Christmas festival, a new birth-festival which will lead us from the present into the times soon to come, when a new Christ-impulse must be born and a new knowledge of the nature of Christ. We need a new understanding of the fact that the divine-spiritual 'heavens' and the physical world of 'earth' are linked to one another, and that the most significant symbol of their union is the Mystery of Golgotha. That is why a warning-message rings out to us, making us aware of the divine-spiritual origin of man, and of the fact that the spiritual revelation of the heavens is inseparable from peace on earth.

The 'holy night' must become a reality. The old-fashioned custom of giving each other presents at Christmas is not enough; the warmth of heart which inspired Christians over the centuries at Christmas has gone. We need a new Christmas, a new 'holy night' — not just reminding us of the birth of Jesus of Nazareth, but actually bringing a new birth, the birth of a new Christ-impulse. In full consciousness, we must learn to understand the supersensible power which was made manifest in the Mystery of Golgotha, was revealed in the material earth. With our full consciousness we must understand what was uttered instinctively in the Mysteries of ancient times. For this impulse we must take into ourselves consciously. It will lead us to understand that when the Christmas 'holy night' becomes a real experience to humanity once more, people will again know the wonderful midnight communion between the revelation of the heavens and the peace of earth.

Notes

1. The Dying God

1. The contents of the Mysteries were a closely guarded secret in the ancient world. However, some sources have survived. They are conveniently collected and presented in Meyer, M.W. (ed.), *The Ancient Mysteries: a Sourcebook,* New York 1987. There is much essential information in Burkert, W., *Ancient Mystery Cults,* London 1987.

2. For Heraclitus and his connection with the Mysteries, see below pp.46ff.

   Steiner points to the great antiquity of the Mysteries, in contrast to many academic authorities who regard them as a late and mixed ('syncretistic') form of religion. Burkert also rightly challenges this 'stereotype,' 'that the mystery religions are "late," that they are typical of late antiquity, that is the Imperial or possibly the later Hellenistic period, when the brilliance of the Hellenic mind was giving way to the irrational' *(op. cit.* p.2). The Mysteries at Eleusis reach back into Mycenaean times (p.8) and had early links to Egypt (pp.20f).

3. Dying and rising gods were known in many of the Mysteries: in the Greek Mysteries there was Dionysus; in the Middle East, Attis and Adonis; in Egypt, Osiris; there are analogies too in Mithraism, which came from the East into the Roman Empire. Often they made use of 'agricultural' imagery, as at Eleusis near Athens. Striking uses of Mystery-language of this kind are found in early Christianity, e.g. 1 Cor 15, 36 ('What you sow does not spring to life unless it dies'), John 12, 24 ('unless a grain of wheat fall into the earth and die ...').

   A classic account — to be treated with some caution — on the 'dying and rising gods' is still Sir J. G. Frazer's *The Golden Bough* (one-volume edition, New York 1947). See further R. Steiner, *The Easter Festival in Relation to the Mysteries,* London 1968.

4. This view was to be taken up and developed by many in twentieth-century theology, but by none more influential than Rudolf Bultmann: cf. his *Kerygma and Myth.* His historical and theological interpretation has dominated Protestant biblical study, and powerfully affected even Catholic approaches. He argued that it was

impossible to get behind the 'legendary' presentation of Jesus presented in the Gospels, and that Christianity's way forward was to
separate the message (*kerygma*, proclamation) from the outmoded
mythological language altogether. Steiner's concept of a Mystery,
which differed from the ancient myths by being centred upon an historical fact, is a far-reaching alternative to this dominant approach.
It requires us rather to go more deeply *into* the nature of the myths,
rather than to shake them off as mere superstition; in that way we
will be able to appreciate how the historical event came to carry the
spiritual meaning, which is the reality that he helps us experience
anew. The inaccessibility of the historical Jesus has only recently
been questioned: see J.H. Charlesworth, *Jesus Within Judaism*, London
1988.

5. Firmicus Maternus, *The Error of the Pagan Religions* translated by C.A.
Forbes, New York 1970, Chapter 22, pp.93f. (Quotation added.) Many
of the details in Steiner's recreation of the event can be confirmed
from the additional account of the Attis-ceremonies in Arnobius of
Sicca, *The Case against the Pagans* V, 5–17.

The identity of the cult concerned in Firmicus continues to be
disputed: some believe (like Forbes) that the god is Osiris rather than
Attis, but a good case for the latter is made out by G. Heuten in his
French version of the *De Errore* (Brussels 1938) and this view is
accepted, e.g. by M.W. Meyer. On the Attis-cult, see further Vermaseren, M.J., *Cybele and Attis: the Myth and the Cult*, London 1977.
The festival took place in spring, from 15 to 27 March. From
evidence in Clement of Alexandria concerning the sacred formulae
of the Mystery, it seems that the worshippers ate from the sacred
drum or tambourine and drank from the cymbal, both attributes of
Attis. Then: 'After a ritual meal, Clement and Firmicus Maternus
would have us believe, the initiate participated in the holiest
ceremonies within a secret, inner chamber and thus became a true
mystes' — i.e. was united with the god (Meyer, M.W., *The Ancient
Mysteries*, San Francisco 1987 p.115; his anthology also includes the
description from Arnobius, pp.116–20).

The symbolic 'lamb' was evidently a woolly fleece, echoing an
episode in the myths of the god: Arnobius V, 16.

6. Underlying Steiner's whole account of man's spiritual history is the
process of the emergence of individuality and intellectual thought,
which ancient humanity did not experience in the way we do today.
Instead, they felt themselves part of the cosmic totality and perceived
its meaning for their lives in pictures, or Imaginations of the spiritual
world. Steiner characterizes these as 'atavistic,' i.e. pertaining to a
prior evolutionary stage of humanity. When they recur in unaltered
form in modern times they are a pathological phenomenon: the
modern path of initiation takes account of the ego-individuality of

man and appeals to the rational thinking that has emerged along with it. Cf. Chapter 7 below. For some of the many accounts by Steiner of atavistic consciousness and the transition to individual thinking, see for instance the early lectures in *The Apocalypse of John* (London, 1977); also *The Christ-Impulse and the Evolution of Ego-Consciousness*, New York 1976.

7. See the range of material in M. Eliade, 'Nostalgia for paradise in the primitive traditions,' in *Myths, Dreams and Mysteries*, London 1968.

8. Steiner is to be understood as objecting to the materialistic interpretation of evolution, not to evolution as such. His own thought is pervasively evolutionary. For Steiner, the emergence of the 'free individual' is the highest stage of evolution, so that the process cannot be without moral significance. He regarded his philosophy as the necessary response to 'the edifice that Darwin and Haeckel have striven to build for natural science. It is the spiritualized theory of evolution carried over into moral life' (*The Philosophy of Freedom*, London 1964 p.169). In a lecture he called for an 'evolutionary' re-interpretation of *The Concepts of Original Sin and Grace*, London 1973.

9. E. Grant Watson writes of 'the potential immortality of all essential cellular elements' of the body — which is demonstrated by the absence of inherent mortality in primitive (unicellular and other) organisms. Thus it is really death which constitutes the biological enigma. He advances the view that mortality is connected with the higher complexity of advanced organisms with all that forms the basis for the soul and the moral life. See Chapter 8 of his *The Mystery of Physical Life*, Edinburgh 1992. (E. Grant Watson was a zoologist influenced both by Steiner and the work of C.G. Jung.)

10. A striking confirmation of the Mystery-view is found in the Babylonian text *Enuma Elish* ('When on high'): there the demoness of death, destruction and chaos is called Tiamat, and the dying, rescued and glorified god is Marduk, the tutelary god of Babylon. The text was recited at an annual festival, and in secret rites the king played the role of the Mystery-god, performing various magical acts to overcome the enemy of life. Of Tiamat it is written:

> let her recede into the future far off from mankind, till time
> is old, keep her forever absent.

After this, Marduk was said to be glorified by the High Gods and became one with the cosmic wisdom-divinity Ea (translated in Sandars, N. K., *Poems of Heaven and Hell from Ancient Mesopotamia*, Harmondsworth 1971, p.10). On the festival, see Borsch, F. H., *The Son of Man in Myth and History*, London 1967, pp.90–100 (with other Near Eastern parallels). Rudolf Steiner knew the Babylonian poem at least in part: versions of it have been available since 1876. He discussed it further in *True and False Paths in Spiritual Investigation*, London 1969, pp.33ff.

11. Such a generalized sense of the persistence of life, different from the later view of personal resurrection, is typical of the Mysteries. Attis survives his ecstatic self-infliction as a mysterious force which brings renewal to nature and to human society (Meyer, M. W., *The Ancient Mysteries* pp.118f; Arnobius V, 7); the Mithras bull dies and renews the world, recreating the primal sacrifice which made the world; etc.

12. Paul, 1 Corinthians 15, 42–44. According to Steiner, this means that the living form of the human body will not be destroyed by the material, perishable substances with which it is clothed. He asserted that esoteric Christian teachings referred explicitly to this living form (*From Jesus to Christ*, London 1991, pp.110ff). His claim was confirmed by the discovery of the early Christian writings from Nag Hammadi, such as the *Gospel of Philip* Saying 23 and the *Letter to Rheginus*. For these, their connections with Paul and with the esoteric conceptions described by Steiner, see further Welburn, A., *Beginnings of Christianity*, Edinburgh 1991, pp.222ff. The concept of a form-body is characterized in both biological and resurrectional terms in Edwards, O., *The Time of Christ*, Edinburgh 1986, pp.176ff; also Weihs, Thomas, *Embryogenesis*, Edinburgh 1986, pp.127ff (both developing Steiner's indications).

2. The Mysteries and their Myths

1. The anthropomorphic nature of human gods was noticed as early as Xenophanes (c.575–480 BC). On his connection with the Mysteries, cf. R. Steiner, *Christianity as Mystical Fact*, London 1972, pp.29–31. There is a good short account of his thought in: Snell, Bruno, The *Discovery of the Mind*, New York 1982, pp.139–43.

2. Alluding to the 'god-making' passage in the Hermetic 'Initiation Discourse' or *Asclepius* 23b: 'Let me tell you, Asclepius, how great is the power and might of man ... Man does not merely receive the light, but also gives it; he not only progresses towards the goal of Godhead, but in truth is a maker of gods ...' On the relationship of this passage to Hermetic ritual and initiation, see Fowden, Garth, *The Egyptian Hermes*, Cambridge 1986, pp.142ff.

   These gods are the familiar ones worshipped by the people, the images in the temples. The initiate does not deny the gods who are present in them; rather he regards their creation as one of man's greatest spiritual achievements.

3. On the Mystery-background of the myths concerning Theseus, see Jeanmaire, H., *Couroï et Courètes*, Lille 1939, pp.323ff.

4. Sallust, *On the Gods and the World* III, 3–4. Sallust's work is conveniently available in Grant, F.C., *Hellenistic Religions*, Indianapolis 1953.

5. This passage is the *locus classicus* of Steiner's mythological 'structural-ism'; cf. similar statements in *The Easter Festival in Relation to the Mysteries*, London 1968, p.13 (on the myths concerning Adonis), and in relation to dream-interpretation, *The Evolution of Consciousness*, London 1966, pp.59f. One may say that for Steiner, equally as for Lévi-Strauss, the study of myth proceeds 'from the study of conscious content to that of unconscious forms' (Lévi-Strauss, *Structural Anthropology*, Harmondsworth 1972, p.24). Through this idea, Steiner was able to recognize the truth expressed in mythologi-cal terms, but without supposing that the mythological consciousness was the sign of a 'primitive mentality' which had to be banished and replaced by rational thought. Rather, as he goes on to say here, the same structures were later embodied in philosophical and indeed scientific thought. Thus Steiner illuminatingly draws our attention to the difference between ancient and modern consciousness, the failure to understand which has cut us off from the sources of ancient wisdom, making us misread them as crude forerunners of modern thought. But he also places both ancient and modern consciousness on a single evolutionary line, linking them in a continuum from mythical through to philosophical thinking. See Chapter 3 below. In a broader sense, this 'evolution of consciousness' provides the perspective for all Steiner's studies in this book.

6. Plotinus, *Enneads* V, 8, 6.

7. *Phaedrus* 229D–230A.

8. On the two horses: *Phaedrus*, 246–257.

9. On the connection of the Osiris-myth with Egyptian divine kingship and the unification of the country, see the brilliant account in Frankfort, Henri, *Kingship and the Gods*, Chicago 1948, especially Chapter 11 ('The Mystery-Play of the Succession'). The Egyptian sources tend to be highly allusive; the main outlines of the myth are to be found in the late Greek author Plutarch, *On Isis and Osiris*. See Steiner's further discussion below pp.90ff; and in *Egyptian Myths and Mysteries*, New York 1971.

10. Empedocles, fragment 26. The main fragments of Empedocles, with English translation and commentary, are available in Kirk-Raven-Schofield, *The Pre-Socratic Philosophers*, Cambridge 1983, pp.280–321. See also below, Chapter 3, Notes 1 and 15.

    For the ambiguous attitude of Empedocles to the emerging rational consciousness, see the remarks of R. Steiner, *The Riddles of Philosophy*, New York 1973, pp.30–32.

11. Empedocles, fragment 20.

12. Empedocles, fragment 109: 'For with earth do we see earth, with water water, with air bright air, with fire consuming fire; with Love do we see Love, Strife with dread Strife.'

13. M. L. West notes the close analogy in particular with the cosmic

Aphrodite of the Orphic Mysteries: *The Orphic Poems*, Oxford 1983, p.92. Further links with Mystery teachings came to light with the discovery, in 1962, of the 'Derveni papyrus,' so-called from the place in Greece where it was found. It contains an Orphic cosmological poem from the sixth century BC, whose mythology sometimes anticipates philosophical ideas, e.g. in the 'startling conception of a god who absorbs the universe and then regenerates it from out of himself' — just like Empedocles' Divine Sphere: West, *op. cit.* p.108. For the dependence of early Greek philosophies on the Mysteries, see Chapter 3 below.

14. Initiation — the attainment of higher consciousness — stands at the heart of all Mysteries, ancient and modern. In ancient times it often took the form of dramatic and harrowing events and ordeals: 'The bodily enactment of these things within the recesses of the Mysteries,' comments Steiner, 'penetrated and transformed the candidate for initiation. It produced an overwhelming impression, a terrible shock in the person's life. Nowadays as we shall see it could not be done in the same way. But such was the ancient form of initiation which stirred to life the inner forces of the soul. It awoke powers of vision which brought him to recognize that he stood no longer in the world of the senses but in the spiritual world' (R. Steiner, *The Easter Festival in Relation to the Mysteries*, p.14). On the inner course of development in the course of initiation, and on the continuities between ancient and modern forms, see R. Steiner, *The Mysteries of the East and Christianity*, London 1972. A valuable study of initiation practices in archaic and other religions is Eliade, M., *Rites and Symbols of Initiation*, New York 1965. For a modern path of initiation: R. Steiner, *Knowledge of Higher Worlds*, London 1969. The Mysteries in fact derive their name from the ancient word for 'initiation.' 'The verbal root *my(s)-* seems to be attested in Mycenaean Greek,' comments W. Burkert, 'possibly for the initiation of an official ... It is more important to note that the word *mysteria* conforms to a well-established type of word formation to designate festivals in Mycenaean ... The [classical Greek] verb *myeo*, 'to initiate' (in the passive, 'to receive initiation') is secondary and indeed much less used than *mystes* and *Mysteria*' (*Ancient Mystery Cults*, Harvard 1987 pp.8f).

15. Details of the voyage already confirm the initiatory character of the quest, e.g. the 'clashing rocks' or Symplegades, a type of the paradoxical or seemingly impassable 'threshold' between this world and the other world. Mircea Eliade writes:

> Let us note that these images emphasize not only the danger of the passage ... but especially the impossibility of imagining that the passage could be made by a being of flesh and blood. The Symplegades show us the paradoxical nature of passage into the beyond, or, more precisely, of transfer from this

world to a world which is transcendent ... The Symplegades
become in some sort 'guardians of the threshold,' homologiz-
able with the monsters and griffins that guard a treasure
hidden at the bottom of the sea, or a miraculous fountain
from which flows the Water of Youth, or a garden in the
midst of which stands the Tree of Life. It is as difficult to
enter the Garden of the Hesperides as it is to pass between
the clashing rocks or to enter a monster's belly. Each of these
exploits constitutes a pre-eminently initiatory ordeal. He who
emerges from such an ordeal victorious is qualified to share
in the superhuman condition — he is a Hero, omniscient,
immortal. (Eliade, M., *Rites and Symbols of Initiation,* pp.65f.)

Aeetes' kingdom was thus originally an otherworldly one,
typically located 'at the end of the earth' beyond the seas, and
Jason's heroic voyage a journey into the beyond comparable to the
journey of the soul after death. The hero–initiate makes that journey
while alive, and returns, bringing with him his 'wife' — cf. the myth
of Orpheus and Eurydice.

16. See below, pp.85ff.

17. The ordinary self as 'dismembered' — an experience that leads on to
the rebirth or liberation of the higher self: these patterns remind us
not only of the myths of the Mysteries concerning Dionysus, Osiris
or Orpheus, but with other strands in the Jason and Medea legends.
There the saga preserves obvious initiatory–shamanic motifs
(shamans-in-the-making dream that they are dismembered, and even
cooked and devoured by divine/demonic beings before being
reconstituted). Medea undertook to rejuvenate Jason's father, Aeson,
on their return to Greece by boiling him in a pot with magical herbs.
Through Medea's trickery, Jason's usurping uncle Pelias was also
chopped up and put in the pot — but without the magical herbs.

18. There is a wide-ranging study of the Prometheus-myth and its
oriental (Vedic, Babylonian) prototypes: Duchemin, J., *Prométhée,*
Paris 1974; Indian analogies are striking especially for the use of fire
(pp.27ff). Rudolf Steiner considered that the Promethean myth was
the expression of an archaic Mystery that had been betrayed. See for
example *The Temple Legend,* London.1985, pp.36–48.

19. The term has a Mystery-connotation: to die 'with good hope' was a
phrase applied to the initiates in the Mysteries of Eleusis, signifying
their knowledge of immortality since they had already died and been
reborn. 'Just as they are called initiations, so in actual fact we have
learned from them the fundamental initiatives of life, and have
grasped the basis not only for living with joy but also for dying with
a better hope' (Cicero, *De legibus* II, 14, 36).

20. A good brief account of the relations, physical and spiritual, between
Eleusis and Athens in Martin, L. H., *Hellenistic Religions,* Oxford 1987,

pp.62–72. On the priestly families, see Clinton, K., *The Sacred Officials of the Eleusinian Mysteries,* Philadelphia 1974. Much evidence is necessarily, considering the secret nature of the Mystery-teachings, iconographical and archaeological: see Bianchi, Ugo, *The Greek Mysteries,* Leiden 1976. Steiner discussed the Eleusinian Mysteries also in *Wonders of the World,* London 1963, and in *Mystery-Knowledge and Mystery-Centres,* London 1973. For such evidence as we have of the contents and sacred formulae of the Mysteries, see Meyer, M. W., *The Ancient Mysteries,* San Francisco 1987, pp.18f, also the important chapter in Eliade, M., *History of Religious Ideas* vol. I, London 1979, pp.290–301.

21. The 'official' account of Demeter at Eleusis is given in the so-called 'Homeric' *Hymn to Demeter*: it is included in Meyer, M. W., *The Ancient Mysteries,* pp.20–30. It was evidently composed around the seventh century BC, and seems to predate the dominance of Athens, speaking only of Eleusis as an independent centre of the Mysteries.

22. Walter Burkert points out that this episode is strikingly close to the Egyptian story of Isis and 'burning Horus,' which had a subsequent history in magic and healing. 'This diffusion of the Egyptian charm and its integration in Egyptian ideology make it unlikely that an origin in Greek literature should be assumed, ... the influence must have come from Egypt to Greece. The reception of the wandering goddess, her power that can be used either for good or for evil, the child in the fire, danger and salvation: these form an impressive and characteristic complex and not just a superficial parallel.' They point to an influence of the Egyptian Mysteries upon the Greek at a very early date — Burkert, W., *Ancient Mystery Cults,* pp.20f. From his own researches, Rudolf Steiner concluded that apart from the stories relating to the Olympians, much of Greek mythology (i.e. the chthonic and Mystery-cult figures) stems from Egypt, and that some lost Egyptian 'myths were preserved for us in the form in which they became domesticated in Greece' (*Egyptian Myths and Mysteries,* p.104; for a specific reference to Isis–Osiris and Eleusis, p.77). This appears to be one example, now rediscovered.

The Mysteries, which aim to unite man with the gods, are quite distinct within the Greek world from the public cults associated with the Olympian gods. The mythology of Olympus, and the 'Delphic theology' which grew from it, stressed the impassable gulf between human and divine.

23. 'The Greeks were conscious that in primaeval times the soul had been gifted with clairvoyance, and they regarded Persephone, the daughter of Demeter, as the ruler of those clairvoyant powers which played into men's souls from the cosmos ... Cosmic forces appeared to them as actual forms or figures, so that men did not speak of abstract forces, but of actual beings. Such a figure as Persephone is

a relic of this consciousness. Through spiritual science we are struggling gradually to come to know again from our modern viewpoint the same living reality in the spiritual world ... the same living beings who lay concealed behind the figures of Greek mythology' (*Wonders of the World*, p.27; these forces have now become unconscious — the subconscious life of the soul, in the 'underworld').

24. He was identified with the mysterious Iacchus, invoked repeatedly in the songs and celebrations of the procession to Eleusis, whose high spirits are wonderfully recreated by Aristophanes (*Frogs* 311–459: excerpted in Meyer, M.W., *The Ancient Mysteries* pp.32–38). His role at Eleusis is obscure, however, although we do know that Eleusinian, Dionysiac and Orphic Mysteries overlapped and interacted in a more complicated way than used to be thought. Steiner described cult-images at Eleusis of a Father-god, surrounded by stars and planets, and a Mother-goddess receiving his fructifying influence. The former reminds us strongly of the Orphic images of the celestial primal-born, Protogonos, later with zodiacal symbolism; the latter of the Eleusinian formula preserved by Hippolytus, 'Rain! Conceive!' (*Refutation of Heresies* V, 7, 34), which Meyer surmises 'was intended as a command to the sky to emit rain and the earth to become fruitful' (op. cit. p.19) He cites, also from Hippolytus, the further formula: 'A holy child is born to the Lady Brimo: Brimos' (V, 8, 40), where Brimo ('Strong One') is evidently Persephone, and the masculine Brimos her child, Dionysus. Dionysus as son of Persephone (rather than of the mortal woman Semele, the usual version) belongs to the specifically Orphic telling of the myth, whose meaning Steiner discusses at length: see *Wonders of the World*, pp.90–101. According to Steiner too, this child-Dionysus or Iacchus was represented on a further cult-image at Eleusis. The candidate for the Mysteries, he says, 'was led into the very holiest place of all. There he had before him the image of the female figure, suckling at her breast the child. And he was led into its meaning with the words, "That is the god Iacchus, who will one day come"...: one who was still a child, a cosmic child, who must first grow up in the cosmos' (*Mystery-Knowledge and Mystery-Centres*, pp.147f). Such representations of Persephone suckling a boy-child (Gk. *kourotrophos*) are rare. One was discovered, however, at the site of a sanctuary of the goddess in Selinus in Sicily — an important centre of her worship — excavated by archaeologists and the results published in 1927. It has prototypes in local styles and now a parallel discovered at Monte Bubbonia near Syracuse. G. Zuntz thus describes the example, in emphatically Greek style, from Selinus and the perplexity it caused to scholarship:

A lovely young woman, seated with a babe in her arms. It stretches a hand up to her breast; she is looking in front of

herself with a forlorn, dreamy gaze. This Greek Madonna:
who is she? Who could she be, at this sanctuary, but Persephone? ... But if so, who, and whose, is the babe? Persephone
kourotrophos: the paradox about the goddess grows ever
more extreme. (Zuntz, *Persephone*, Oxford 1971, p.151.)

25. Steiner's remarks are obviously to be applied, not to the literary epic,
but to the mythical-heroic narrative which underlies it. Comparable
instances are the *Epic of Gilgamesh*, and the *Aeneid*. All of them have
clear initiatory structures in their main outlines.

3. From Myth to Philosophy — the pre-Socratics

1. This view has been supported by a number of eminent scholars since
Steiner's time: see notably the account of F.M. Cornford, 'Mystery-
religions and pre-Socratic philosophy' in *Cambridge Ancient History*
IV, Cambridge 1939. A number of discoveries, particularly relating
to the Orphic mysteriosophical teachings, have confirmed the connection — several of them will be mentioned in the notes. Some of
the standard presentations still resist the force of the conclusions. For
example, Kirk-Raven-Schofield, *The Presocratic Philosophers*, Cambridge 1983, insists, 'The relevance of Orphic beliefs is still, even in
the light of the new evidence, fairly slight ... ' (p.33); but the
discoveries have basically confirmed that Mystery-ideas were
sufficiently developed by the sixth century BC to play the sort of role
which Steiner describes. It has been argued in particular that a
widespread synthesis of religious-philosophical ideas in the East,
originating in Egypt and influencing thought as far away as the
India of the Upanishads, provided the groundwork of concepts
concerning Eternity (*Aion*, Unageing Time, 'Time without shore,' etc.)
and a mythical cosmogony. This synthesis affected emergent Greek
thought: West, M.L., *Early Greek Philosophy and the Orient*, Oxford
1971. That the teachings were already known in the Greek Mysteries
is proved by the 'Derveni papyrus' (text and translation in Kirk-
Raven-Schofield, pp.31f), which preserves an Orphic poem on the
Creation from the sixth century BC. It contains many concepts
reminiscent of the pre-Socratic philosophers, such as Parmenides and
Empedocles, but West's analysis shows clearly that in the case of
Empedocles, at least, the poem is prior: 'The Orphic narrative
provides a mythical prototype for his philosophical vision,' while the
evidence from Parmenides points, if not to dependency, then to 'a
single stream from which both drew' — West, M.L., *The Orphic
Poems*, Oxford 1983, pp.108, 110. The poem may originally have
begun with the line 'I sing to those with understanding,' which uses
the same vocabulary as Heraclitus (fragment 1). The poem has

striking similarities to the thought of Pherecydes of Syros; for Steiner on his Orphic Mystery-connection, see below pp.62ff (especially 65). For the special case of Plato, see next chapter.

At the other end of the scale, it is important to realize that the pre-Socratics opened up philosophical issues that are still with us: cf. Popper, Karl, 'Back to the Presocratics' in his *Conjectures and Refutations*, London 1969; Barnes, Jonathan, *The Presocratic Philosophers*, London 1982.

2. Plato, *Phaedo* 69C.

The Mystery-formula which Plato cites contrasts the mass of worshippers who at the Dionysiac festivals carried the wand or thyrsus, the emblem of the god, and those few who are joined with his divine nature through initiation and are themselves a Bacchus. In the language of the Mysteries, the initiate is often said to 'become an Osiris,' an Attis, an Adonis, and so on. In the new discoveries of texts from Nag Hammadi, which document the connection between the Mysteries and early Christianity, we find the Mystery-language strikingly reapplied, this time to the Christian aspirant. Both the Gospel of Thomas and the Gospel of Philip refer to the attainment of mystic union in Mystery-terms as 'marriage,' and the latter to a rite of the Marriage Chamber or higher Christian initiation. Of those who have been through it, the Gospel of Philip says: 'This one is no longer a Christian, but a Christ' (Saying 67). Gospel of Thomas Saying 75 ('Many are standing at the door, but the unified ones are those who shall enter the Marriage Chamber') echoes the Mystery-formula which Plato quoted in its ancient Greek form.

3. *Palatine Anthology* IX-540; Diogenes Laertius, *Lives* IX, 16. According to Steiner, the *Logos*-doctrine taught by Heraclitus had roots in the Mysteries of the Ephesian Artemis, and these latter were concerned with sacred speech and the origins of the universe. He pointed out that when the *Logos* appears again, in Christianity, it is in the Gospel of John — and the figure of John is associated in tradition and legend with Ephesus too; R. Steiner, *Mystery-Knowledge and Mystery-Centres*, London 1973, pp.81ff. Heraclitus certainly presents his teaching on the *Logos* as one which cannot be grasped by the profane:

> Of the *Logos* as I describe it, men always prove to be
> uncomprehending — [that is the Orphic Mystery-language]
> — both before they have heard it and when once they have
> heard it. For although all things happen in accordance with
> this *Logos*, men are like people of no experience ... when I
> distinguish each thing according to its constitution and
> declare how it is; the rest of men fail to notice what they do
> after they wake up as surely as they do when they are
> asleep. (fragment 1)

Steiner referred to the pioneering work of Pfleiderer, E., *Die Philosophie des Heraklit,* Berlin 1886.

4. Plutarch, *On the E at Delphi* 392B. Cf. Heraclitus fragments 12 and 91.
    The chief fragments of Heraclitus are available in Kirk-Raven-Schofield, *The Presocratic Philosophers,* pp.181–212. On the summation (rather than actual saying) 'All is in flux,' pp.185f.

5. That is, he was not, as is usually supposed, expressing a pessimistic and merely relativistic point of view. Cf. below p.65.

6. Fragment 88.

7. Fragment 78A (Bywater).

8. Fragment 15; and cf. fragment 49A.
    Recent discoveries confirm Steiner's conclusion that Heraclitus was drawing on the Mysteries. Archaeological investigations at Olbia, on the Black Sea coast, in 1951 yielded a number of bone tablets — possibly membership tokens of an Orphic-Bacchic Mystery, dating from around the fifth century BC. One of them has scratched upon it an abbreviation of Dionysus, then the words 'Orphics' and 'Life-Death-Life.' Another one, again with the abbreviated form of 'Dionysus,' has 'War-Peace Truth-Falsehood.' See further West, M.L., *The Orphic Poems,* pp.17ff (with line reproductions of the tablets); and for their relevance to Heraclitus, Kirk-Raven-Schofield, *The Presocratic Philosophers,* pp.208, 210.

9. Fragments 110f.

10. Fragment 61.

11. Fragment 51.

12. Fragment 62.

13. Fragment 52.

14. The main passages on 'fire' are collected in Kirk-Raven-Schofield, *The Presocratic Philosophers,* pp.197–99. Cf. Steiner's analysis of Pherecydes' thought, pp.62ff below.

15. Fragment 119. Similar ideas are to be found in other pre-Socratics, but they have not been grasped by many modern historians of thought, who treated them as allegories of impersonal 'reason,' etc. A notable exception is E.R. Dodds, who discusses the notion of the *psyche* entombed in the body: 'To people who equated the psyche with the empirical personality ... it was a fantastic paradox ... Nor does it make much better sense if we equate "soul" with reason. I should suppose that for people who took it seriously what lay "dead" within the body was neither the reason nor the empirical man, but an "occult self," Pindar's "image of life," which is indestructible but can function only in the exceptional conditions of sleep or trance. That man has two "souls," one of divine, the other of earthly origin, was already taught ... by Pherecydes of Syros. And it is significant that Empedocles ... avoids applying the term *psyche* to the indestructible self. He appears to have thought of the *psyche*

as being the vital warmth which at death is reabsorbed in the fiery element from which it came (that was a fairly common fifth-century view). The occult self which persisted through successive incarnations he called, not *psyche*, but "daemon". This daemon has, apparently, nothing to do with perception or thought, which Empedocles held to be mechanically determined; the function of the daemon is to be the carrier of man's potential divinity and actual guilt. It is nearer in some ways to the indwelling spirit which the shaman inherits from other shamans than it is to the rational "soul" in which Socrates believed; but it has been moralized as a guilt-carrier, and the world of the senses has become the Hades in which it suffers torment ... The complementary aspect of the doctrine was its teaching on the subject of catharsis — the means whereby the occult self might be advanced on the ladder of being, and its eventual liberation hastened' *(The Greeks and the Irrational,* Berkeley, 1951, pp.152f).

16. Cf. below, pp.61ff. Reincarnation formed an important part of Orphic mysteriosophy in Greece, and the idea is taken up by several early philosophers. It is now generally accepted that this was not a 'speculation,' but goes back to experiences of remembering other lives, as is still done by shamans — the last inheritors of the ancient initiatory wisdom and its techniques. Rudolf Steiner described the origins of Orphism from a bardic-shamanic culture in Europe, whose ideas evidently reached Greece via Thrace, the region associated with Orpheus: see *The Christ-Impulse and the Evolution of Ego-Consciousness,* New York 1976, pp.18ff. The shamanic origins of Orphism are accepted by M.L. West and many other scholars today; cf. especially Dodds, E.R., *The Greeks and the Irrational* pp.135–78. Steiner points out below how Pythagoras too 'linked on to archaic doctrines' (see p.61 and accompanying note 28). The doctrines spread through Europe, meaning perhaps the Black Sea coastal region (cf. the discoveries at Olbia) from Central Asia.

   Rudolf Steiner, of course, did not believe in reincarnation on the basis of 'archaic doctrines.' See the approach to his concept of human destiny in Chapter 2 ('The Re-embodiment of the Spirit') of his *Theosophy,* London 1965.

17. Empedocles, fragment 11.
18. Empedocles, fragment 12.
19. Empedocles, fragment 15. All three fragments are passages from his lost poem *On Nature.*
20. Cf. fragment 112, which describes the destiny of those who rise through the cycle of lives to become 'heroes,' 'bards' etc.: 'And thence they arise as gods, highest in honour; sharing with the other immortals their hearth and their table, without part in human sorrows or weariness.' Kirk-Raven-Schofield note that here Empedocles 'is probably drawing also on the eschatology of the Pythagorean

mystery-religion' (p.317) and quote for comparison the beautiful fragment of Pindar which refers to it (quoted by Plato, *Meno* 81B). They also compare the language of the Orphic gold plates from Thurii which greet the initiate in the other world with the words 'Happy and blessed one, you shall be a god instead of a mortal' (p.314). Similar ideas in epitaphs from fifth century BC onward: in Lindsay, J., *Origins of Astrology*, London 1971, pp.92–95, 235f.

21. Steiner's philosophical writings are devoted to overcoming the assumptions contained in the on-looker mentality, and developing an approach to knowledge which sees man as a part of the world-order he knows — indeed as a key to it. That is his 'anthroposo-phical' approach, which has been echoed in interesting ways recently in the 'anthropic' views which are also beginning to challenge the dominance of the on-looker assumption. See R. Steiner, *Truth and Knowledge*, New York 1981; *The Philosophy of Freedom*, London 1964.

22. Pindar, fragment 102.

23. Aristotle, *Metaphysics* 985b24–34. Pythagoras himself wrote nothing. His pupils attributed many doctrines to him, and many stories were circulated about him. Hence he is inescapably entangled in legend and rumour. The main evidence about him is given in Kirk-Raven-Schofield, *The Presocratic Philosophers*, pp.214–38. Efforts to rescue a 'biography' from the mists can hardly be called successful; but some solid information remains. Typical of many initiates would be the extensive travels: Pythagoras is said to have journeyed e.g. to Babylon, where he learned the wisdom of the Chaldaean Zaratas (Hippolytus, *Refutation* I, 2, 12).

23a. A fine study of the Pythagorean teachings, including their Mystery-shamanic elements, is: Burkert, W., *Lore and Science in Ancient Pythagoreanism*, Harvard 1972. 'In considering the ultimate origins of star-observation and theories of the heavens,' notes J. Lindsay, 'we may note further that the shamanist ritual-mime of sky-ascent has it-self the background of initiation experience ... Early Pythagorean ideas are hard to make out clearly, in themselves or their origins. But certainly they owed much to various Eastern sources ... The Pythago-rean Harmony of the Spheres assumed that the distances between the planetary spheres have the ratios of simple whole numbers, and this kind of speculation was quite probably linked with, and derived from, Babylonian cosmology' (*Origins of Astrology*, London 1971, pp.93ff).

24. Gregory of Nyssa, *Oratio catechetica magna*, 10.

25. Kirk-Raven-Schofield also conclude that 'there must have been considerable similarity between Pythagorean practice and that described as Orphic' (*The Presocratic Philosophers*, p.221).

26. Cf. Porphyry, *Life of Pythagoras* 19: 'What he said to his associates, nobody can say for certain; for silence with them was of no ordinary kind.'

27. The evidence is collected in Kirk-Raven-Schofield, *The Presocratic Philosophers* pp.219f. The reincarnating entity in his teaching was probably called *psyche*.

28. E.R. Dodds suggested one possible link: 'We know at any rate,' he wrote:

> that Pythagoras founded a kind of religious order, a community of men and women whose rule of life was determined by the expectation of lives to come. Possibly there were precedents ... we may remember the Thracian Zalmoxis in Herodotus, who assembled 'the best of the citizens' and announced to them, not that the human soul is immortal, but that *they and their descendants* were going to live for ever — they were apparently chosen persons, a sort of spiritual *élite*. That there was some analogy between Zalmoxis and Pythagoras must have struck the Greek settlers in Thrace, from whom Herodotus heard the story, for they made Zalmoxis into Pythagoras' slave. That was absurd, as Herodotus saw: the real Zalmoxis was a daemon, possibly a heroized shaman of the distant past. But the analogy was not so absurd ... *(The Greeks and the Irrational,* p.166 n61.)

See further Eliade, M., *Salmoxis: the Vanishing God,* Chicago 1972.

29. A generally neglected figure of the sixth century BC. A book, called *Heptamuchos* ('The Seven Recesses') is attributed to him. Fragments of it survive in quotation: see Kirk-Raven-Schofield, *The Presocratic Philosophers,* pp.50–71. Steiner was highly unusual in attributing to him an important role in the emergence of thought, but opinion has increasingly given him prominence. See the recent remarks of Schibli, H.S., *Pherecydes of Syros,* Oxford 1990.

Tradition also assigns to him a *Theology,* which may or may not be a separate work.

30. That is, no difference is made by earlier modes of consciousness between the inner ('spiritual') world of thoughts and external things. In Steiner's day, anthropologists called this animism, or projection, by human beings, of soul qualities on to natural objects. Steiner denied this. He pointed out that in young children we find a lack of differentiation between self and world: 'The child does not see the table as ensouled. He does not yet feel a soul in himself, but regards himself ... on the same level as the table he bangs' *(Egyptian Myths and Mysteries,* New York 1971, pp.31f; ideas like Steiner's have become widely accepted, see for example Piaget, J., *The Child's Conception of the World,* London 1973). Ancient man did not experience separateness either, though his consciousness was in its own way much more highly developed than that of a modern child, which presents no more than a vestige of the archaic picture-

consciousness. In primitive humanity, this was still a sort of clairvoyance. For instance, when looking at a pond:

> Simply through looking at it, he would have felt whether the water was sweet or salty. It was not at all like our seeing water today. We see only the surface and do not penetrate into the inner qualities. But while a dim clairvoyance still prevailed, the man who approached the pond had no alien feeling towards it. He felt himself as being within the properties of the water; he did not stand over against the object as we do; it was as though he could penetrate into the water. (R. Steiner, *Egyptian Myths and Mysteries*, p.30.)

Pherecydes' Zeus, Chronos and Chthon — or in his dialect Greek: Zas, Chronos and Chthonie — are less 'concepts' than picture-experiences which straddle the gulf, as it seems to us, between thoughts and actual things. For Pherecydes, that gulf did not exist; or, he just begins to notice it, standing at a delicate moment of transition in the history of human awareness.

31. Steiner's statement was first fully corroborated by the modern discoveries of Orphic texts. From these M.L. West argued the existence, by the beginning of the sixth century BC, of 'a newly evolved cosmogonic myth to the effect that Time was the first god, and that he generated out of his seed the materials for the world's creation ... The influence of this myth ... is to be seen in one of the earliest of Greek prose works, the *Theology* of Pherecydes of Syros, in which the god Time was represented as creating out of his own seed. We can now recognize the myth in the Orphic cosmogony' (*The Orphic Poems*, p.104). The most important of the new sources was the Derveni papyrus (cf. above Chapter 2, note 12).

32. Lit. 'the best' *(ariston):* as reported in Aristotle, *Metaphysics* 1091b10.

4. Platonic Mysteries

1. On this question, see Ross, W.D., *Plato's Theory of Ideas*, Oxford 1951, which devotes several chapters to the famous and obscure 'unwritten doctrines.'

2. The genuineness of the Seventh Letter is argued convincingly by Morrow, G.R., *Plato's Epistles*, Indianapolis 1962, pp.44f.

3. *Seventh Letter* 341B–D.

4. For Plato's views on the inadequacy of written language to the processes of philosophical inquiry, see *Phaedrus* 274B–277. The main statement of his ideas on true speech and the speaking of poetry comes in the *Ion*. In real terms, comments J. Wolfgang Ernst, 'this work has been one of the most influential in world literature, far more so than the celebrated *Poetics* of Aristotle, and comparable only to the *Elements* of Euclid' (*Ion. Die Kunst, Dichtung zu sprechen,*

Freiburg im Breisgau 1975, p.7). Plato's affirmation of 'presence' in the spoken word is nowadays accepted as the central philosophical statement on meaning in Western culture — both by those who accept and those who argue against it. Cf. further, *Seventh Letter* 343A–344B.

5. *Phaedo* 58E–59A.
6. *Phaedo* 64A.
7. *Phaedo* 64D–65A.
8. *Phaedo* 65A–B.
9. 'Thus for Plato the whole world changes into ideas that act upon each other. Their effect in the world is produced through the fact that the ideas are reflected in *hyle* (primal matter). What we see as the many individual things and events comes to pass through this reflection. Our need is not to extend knowledge to the original *hyle*, however, for in it there is no truth. We reach the True only if we strip the world-picture of everything that is not idea' — R. Steiner, *The Riddles of Philosophy*, New York 1973, p.39.
10. *Phaedo* 65E–66A.
11. *Phaedo* 67D–E.
12. *Phaedo* 68C.
13. 'In Plato thought has become bold enough not merely to point towards the soul but to define it, so to speak, and describe what it is. What thought has to say about the soul gives it the power of knowing itself in the eternal ... The soul perceives thought. As the soul appears in earthly life it could not produce in itself the pure forms of thought. Where then does the thought-experience come from, if it cannot be developed in earthly life? It represents the recollection of a pre-earthly, purely spiritual state of being. Thought ... has been revealed to the soul in an earlier state of being (pre-existence) in the spiritual world (world of ideas) and the soul recalls it during its terrestrial existence through reminiscence of the life it has spent in the spirit' — R. Steiner, *The Riddles of Philosophy*, p.40. Steiner himself was, of course, not a philosophical Platonist; however, for an anthroposophical perspective on the reality behind these ideas, see his *Study of Man*, London 1966, pp.27ff. In this context Plato's use of myth falls into place. The Mystery-knowledge led to visions of the afterlife, and, although Plato does not believe it possible to prove them by reason, yet, given that 'the soul evidently is immortal' (*Phaedo* 114d) there is 'something natural about assuming ... the outlines of eschatological judgment and bliss, sketched in Orphic-Pythagorean mythology ... For if one is persuaded by the *Phaedo*'s arguments, then to disregard such pictures is to risk eternal ill, while to accept them and be moved by them is possibly to gain salvation ... there is no tension between Plato's commitment to logos and rational enquiry, on the one hand, and his

use of mythos, on the other. In the *Phaedo* especially, the latter naturally grows out of his arguments for the soul's immortality' (Morgan, M.L., *Platonic Piety: Philosophy and Ritual in Fourth-Century Athens*, New Haven 1990, pp.74f). Detailed parallels between Plato's myths and the Orphic-Pythagorean tradition are listed in P. Frutiger, *Les mythes de Platon*, Paris 1930, pp.254–60.

14. *Phaedo* 79D–81A.

15. *Phaedo* 106B.

16. If M.L. Morgan is right, Plato could have inherited such an approach from Socrates. He reconstructs Socrates' connection with the Corybantic rites which belonged to the Mysteries of Dionysus, arguing that he encountered them (and may have been initiated) during his period of military service in Macedonia (near Thrace). Socrates is 'attracted by the lofty, central place given to the soul and the conception of a human struggle to cure it and seek its divinity, repelled by the hysteria and the irrationality of the rites and the cults. Adapting these traditions, together with his unique method of sophistic examination and rational inquiry, Socrates develops a rational revision of ecstatic ritual based on the conviction that human beings can attain divine status' (*Platonic Piety: Philosophy and Ritual in Fourth-Century Athens*, p.30). Morgan further argues that Plato developed his own method from that of Socrates, under the further influence of Orphic-Pythagorean ideas (pp.38ff).

17. *Timaeus* 27C–D.

18. *Timaeus* 48D.

19. *Timaeus* 22C–D. This myth, like most of those in the *Timaeus*, suggests less the world of the Greek cosmogonic myths (Hesiod's *Theogony* etc.), which Plato virtually ignores, and more the account in Genesis; in later times Plato was called a 'Moses speaking the Attic tongue.' Obvious grounds for comparison are:

Timaeus	Genesis
World 'created' by a Demiurge or 'craftsman' God ('Father')	World 'created' by God, the divine Father
Story of Phaethon ('Shiner'), his aspiration to ascend to heaven, his punishment	Story of Lucifer ('Light bearer')
Story of the sinful peoples of Atlantis and its destruction by Flood	Story of sinful peoples of the world and the Flood
World is 'a moving image of Eternity'; man's head is made spherical 'in imitation of the circular figure of the universe'	World is made for man to rule; man is made in the image of the eternal God

Both traditions are evidently a refraction of Mysteries, synthesised from the sixth century BC onwards, concerning an Eternal Being (*Aion,* Zervan, etc; cf. Chapter 3, note 1 above) transcending the world, which is however an 'image' or 'product' of his nature. In the Iranian version, his Son is called 'Creator' and this as well as Egyptian myth may directly have influenced Genesis; a parallel God Olam ('Eternity') is found in a sixth-century Phoenician cosmogony too, with many close parallels to Genesis.

These ideas came to Plato through the Orphic Mysteries of Greece: see West, M.L. *The Orphic Poems,* Oxford 1983, pp.103ff. The modern discoveries which have permitted the reconstruction of the Time-Eternity cosmologies of the Mysteries thus confirm Steiner's view that Plato was giving further philosophical expression to a Mystery teaching.

Steiner points out with respect to Pherecydes (above, p.65) that this development in the teaching of the Mysteries corresponds to a step forward in consciousness, leading to a deeper apprehension of God as transcending the natural world in which he had hitherto revealed himself, and of which the emergence of rational thought is one important aspect. The rationalizing and bringing into the open of such teachings did not go unopposed: already in Antiquity, Plato was accused of having 'stolen' his doctrines from Mystery sources. See Taylor, A.E., *A Commentary on Plato's Timaeus,* Oxford 1928, pp.39–41.

20. *Timaeus* 28C.
21. *Timaeus* 92C
22. Philo, *De legum allegoria* I, 19. Philo's time is that of Christian origins. His work consists of philosophical (platonizing) commentaries on the books of the Bible. See further R. Steiner, *Christianity as Mystical* Fact, London 1972, pp.137–40. Peder Borgen comments on Philo's concept of the *Logos* as joining God and human beings:

> Philo's technical use of the term *Logos* connotes God's mental activity during the act of creating. The *Logos,* one of the powers of the intelligible world, reaches into our world, mainly through the mediators Moses and Aaron, both called *Logos* ... In another sense, the *Logos* and *logoi* may be conceived as heavenly figures such as angels and archangels. The *Logos* is also called a 'second God,' or 'God's first-born' (in M.E. Stone, ed., *Jewish Writings of the Second Temple Period,* Assen 1984, p.273).

23. Philo, *De confusione linguarum* 63.
24. Philo, *De posteritate Caini* 101f.
25. See the detailed study by Goodenough, E. R., *By Light, Light: the Mystic Gospel of Hellenistic Judaism,* New Haven 1935 — a work still regarded as controversial. Also, especially for links to the Mysteries of Isis and Osiris, Mack, B. L., *Logos und Sophia,* Göttingen 1973.

26. Philo, *De migratione Abrahami* 34f.

27. Philo, *Quod a Deo mittantur somnia* II, 323.

28. Philo, *De legum allegoria* III, 29.

29. Hippolytus, *Refutation* V, 8, 9. On the Samothracian Mysteries, see the archaeological evidence and other material in Lehmann, K. and Lewis, N., *Samothrace*, New York 1958; short accounts in Meyer, M. W., *The Ancient Mysteries*, San Francisco 1987, pp.38ff. See further R. Steiner, *Mystery-Knowledge and Mystery-Centres*, London 1973, pp.167–79.

    On the 'Man' figure more generally, in the ancient Near East, the Mysteries and Christianity: much interesting material in Borsch, F. H. *The Son of Man in Myth and History*, London 1967 (p.182 for the passage from Hippolytus).

30. F. M. Cornford argued that the background of the 'Mystery of Love' lay in the Eleusinian Mysteries: see 'The doctrine of Eros in Plato's *Symposium*' in Guthrie, W. K. C., *The Unwritten Philosophy and Other Essays*, Cambridge 1967. Steiner's remarks on Eros in the Eleusinian setting (see *Wonders of the World, Ordeals of the Soul, Revelations of the Spirit*, London 1963, pp.19f) suggest a similar perspective.

31. That is not to reject the analogy with Eleusis. M.L. Morgan accepts also the Dionysiac element, arguing not only that the evidence points to a presence of Dionysus at Eleusis in Plato's time (cf. Steiner, p.41 above and accompanying note 24), but that the Eleusinian institution- alized Mysteries were a mediate stage between the Bacchic ecstasy of the maenads and the rational mind — *Platonic Piety: Philosophy and Ritual in Fourth-Century Athens*, p.99. Steiner here cites the specifically Orphic version of the Dionysus-myth, suggesting once more that it was the esoteric understanding of the myths in the Mysteries rather than the popular forms which determined Plato's thought.

32. The initiatory interpretation of the Orphic Dionysus-myth is argued in detail in West, M. L. *The Orphic Poems*, Oxford 1983, pp.143ff. He argues that a fusion of the 'shamanic' Mysteries with other initiation rites from the Dionysus-cult of Crete took place, reaching Athens in the last third of the fifth century BC. He notes the mention by Plato of the Corybantic rites in this context (pp.174f). We may see here a meeting of the two types (or 'streams') within the Mysteries, which Steiner often distinguished as the 'northern' or ecstatic (cf. shaman- ism) and the 'southern' or Mysteries of descent into one's inner nature. See *Macrocosm and Microcosm*, London 1968, pp.54ff. A fusion of the two was only fully achieved in Christianity.

5. From the Mysteries to Christianity

1. A modern English rendering is available: *The Ancient Egyptian Book of the Dead* translated by R. Faulkner, London 1985.

   Still more archaic discoveries, such as the *Pyramid Texts* (c.2500–2300 BC), show the antiquity of 'astral immortality' among the Egyptians. 'After death,' as Eliade summarizes their beliefs in the earliest period, 'souls made their way to the stars and shared in their eternity. The sky was imagined as a Mother Goddess, and death was equivalent to a new birth, in other words to a rebirth in the sidereal world' *(A History of Religious Ideas, London 1979, p.94.)* He notes that these ideas, as applied to the Pharaoh, 'presuppose ... initiation, including certain rituals and teachings (funerary mythology and geography, secret formulae, etc.). The few allusions found in the *Pyramid Texts* constitute the earliest written documents having to do with obtaining a privileged destiny by virtue of certain secret kinds of knowledge. We here undoubtedly have an immemorial heritage, also shared by the predynastic Neolithic cultures' (p.96n32). The *Pyramid Texts* were followed by the *Coffin Texts* and finally by the *Book of the Dead* (p.111).

1. On the sense in which Egyptian cults and initiations can rightly be called Mysteries, cf. Meyer, M.W., *The Ancient Mysteries,* San Francisco 1987, pp.157f and the important study of 'The Mystery-play of the succession' in Frankfort, H., *Kingship and the Gods,* Chicago 1948, Chapter 11.

2. See above, pp.31ff.

3. *Book of the Dead,* Chapter 125; cf. Faulkner 1985, p.33. Steiner follows the Papyrus of Nu.

4. *Book of the Dead,* Chapter 125; Faulkner p.33 renders: 'lower part of the papyrus plant.'

5. At first, the living of a higher life is undertaken only by the Pharaoh. Later, the Mysteries were 'democratized' by being opened to nobles and eventually to others who were called to them. On the special role of the Pharaoh, see the fine study from an anthroposophical viewpoint: Teichmann, F., *Die Kultur der Empfindungsseele,* Stuttgart 1990.

6. Plato, *Timaeus* 36B–37A; above, pp.80f.

7. Our main source for the Mysteries of Isis and Osiris is the strange and fascinating novel by Apuleius, *The Golden Ass* or *Metamorphoses.* It combines fantasy with autobiography and a spiritual message, culminating in the veiled description of the Mystery-rites. Initiation is compared with 'a voluntary death' as well as with birth. Of his experiences in the Mysteries, Apuleius says:

   I entered the confines of death, and crossed the threshold of Persephone; I was caught rapt through all the elements; I

saw the sun shining at midnight with a brilliant light; I
beheld the upper and the lower gods, drew near and adored.
See, I have told my experience, and yet what you hear can
mean nothing to you. (XI, 23)

Steiner discussed these experiences at length in his lectures on *The
Mysteries of the East and Christianity*, London 1972.

8. Cf. Apuleius, *The Golden Ass* XI, 24 (his higher Osiris-initiation). In
the Mysteries this 'exalted' experience was sometimes termed a
'glorification': see Reitzenstein, R., *Die hellenistischen Mysterienreli-
gionen*, Leipzig 1927, pp.228f. For connections with Christianity:
Welburn, A., *Beginnings of Christianity*, Edinburgh 1991, pp.265ff.

9. The cult of the god Mithra (in Latin or Greek, Mithras) was much
older, and was known in ancient India and especially in Iran. It was
from Iran that it reached the West, where it retained many Persian
features despite considerable changes. Its central act was the slaying
of a bull, and the communicants of the Mystery were admitted to a
sacred meal. The most informative account available in English is:
Vermaseren, M. J., *Mithras, the Secret God*, London 1963. Initiation
took place through seven stages, leading to union with the god. Each
had an elaborate symbolism and meaning, see below and Vermaseren, pp.141ff.

Attempts to deny the real continuity of the Mithraic Mysteries and
the older Mithras-cults are often made; but it is more accurate to
speak of the older cult structures being overlaid by Hellenistic and
other ideas. See the example in Burkert, W., *Ancient Mystery Cults*,
Harvard 1987, pp.83f.

10. Since Steiner's time, philology has established that the name Mithra
originally meant 'bond, or agreement' in the ancient language of Iran
(old Avestan). R. Merkelbach explains:

It has been established that the Persian word *mithra* has the
meaning 'bond.' Thus the god bore a significant name, and
was himself the embodiment of the basis of society, the
personal connections formed by agreement between
individual human beings. This function remained part of the
meaning of the Mithraic cult for the Roman Mithras
Mysteries too. (*Mithras*, Königstein 1984, p.*vii*.)

See further Merkelbach pp.23ff for an analysis of the Persian social
order, in which Mithra guarded the pledges of obedience to the Shah
and his representatives. The Shah (or King, Emperor) who stands at
the pinnacle and so is the ground of society itself, might aspire to be
a kind of avatar of Mithra, as did Cyrus the Great (pp.31ff).

11. 'The second grade of initiation, that of the so-called Occultist,
involved something inimical to the man of today. "Occult" means
concealed hidden, and at this stage the neophytes were no longer
sent out into the world. They learned something that is no longer

taught today: being silent. In the ancient Mysteries learning to be silent constituted a definite stage in the teaching and, grotesque as it may appear to some, they spent a year or more in which they had to be silent. And through being silent they learned an incredible amount ... In silence, things make an extremely strong impression, and the result is that the inner being of man begins to speak to him. It is as though you were to have a basin and a flow of water out of it. Unless there is a spring, a constant source, the basin will run dry. And so it is with man's constant talking. Everything flows away and runs out; nothing remains within. In Antiquity this was understood, and it was for that reason that the pupils in the Mysteries had silence imposed upon them. First they were taught to value truth, then to be silent.' (R. Steiner, *Die Geschichte der Menschheit und die Weltanschauungen der Kulturvölker*, Dornach 1950, pp.41f.)

12. The Mithraic use of the term *kryphios* remains obscure. Its application to the second grade in the *Letters* of St Jerome was no more than a conjecture by the editors von Hilbert and Labourt — see R. Merkelbach, *Mithras*, Königstein 1984, p.77n2. The name normally given to one of the second grade was *nymphus*. Vermaseren concludes that the 'occultists' were in some obscure way closely connected with the second grade — Vermaseren, M.J., *Mithras, the Secret God*, p.139.

13. 'At the fifth stage, the initiates were charged to speak only out of the common spirit. They were known by the name of the people to which they belonged — Persians, Indians or Greeks. It was through the Mysteries that true "Greeks" came into existence ... By the time he reached the fifth grade, the *mystes* no longer had any special wishes of his own, apart from those of the community; he made them his own. Thus he became a kind of "spirit of the people." In the ancient Mysteries, including those in Greece, these "spirits of the people" were men of great wisdom.' (R. Steiner, *Die Geschichte der Menschheit und die Weltanschauungen der Kulturvölker*, p.44.)

14. 'The sixth grade was reached when the initiate no longer had an earthly perspective — not even that of the community. He saw himself, for instance, as a Greek with brother-initiates of the fifth grade who were Syrians in Syria or Persians in the lands a little farther off. But he now regarded all their standpoints as limited. The sun, however, travels over Persia towards Greece, and shines upon us all. The initiates of the sixth grade therefore aspired to learn, not what a particular people had to say, but what the sun had to say. They became Sun-men (*heliodromoi*, lit. "runners with the sun").

'They were no longer men of the earth, but of the sun. And they tried to discover the sun-perspective on things. This is scarcely intelligible to people today, who no longer have an idea of the Mystery-knowledge ... The Sun-men investigated the Mysteries of the sun. Thus in the Pyramids, which were not just built as tombs for the Pharaohs, there were exact openings which allowed the rays of the sun to enter at a specific time of the year. The sun's rays traced a pattern on the ground, which they studied and from which they drew inspiration. In such ways were the living Mysteries of the sun researched. The Sun-man no longer orientated himself towards earthly things, but towards the sun. And then, after a period as a Sun-man when the initiate had learned to orientate himself towards things beyond the earth, he would be exalted to the rank of a Father (pater). This was the highest rank, attained by few. They were the mature leaders to whom all owed allegiance — in the first place because of their ripe years, since by the time the seventh grade was reached the initiate would have grown old — and in addition because of their life's wisdom.' (R. Steiner, Die Geschichte der Menschheit und die Weltanschauungen der Kulturvölker, pp.45–48.)

15. For a description of the bloody sacrifice or taurobolium, through which the initiate was 'reborn into eternity,' see the account by Prudentius, translated in Meyer, M.W., The Ancient Mysteries, pp.128–30. In this form the ritual came into Mithraism from the ecstatic cults of Asia Minor. On the original meaning of the bull-sacrifice for the Mithraic initiates, see R. Steiner, Michaelmas and the Soul-Forces of Man, New York 1982, pp.43–47.

For the cultic meal of the Mithraists, which was associated with an 'image' or perhaps enactment of resurrection (imaginem resurrectionis) see Vermaseren, M.J., Mithras, the Secret God, pp.103ff. Similarities to the Christian eucharist so worried the orthodox Fathers that they had to invent a bizarre theory. The Devil had parodied Christian rites in advance in the pagan Mysteries!

On the elements from Eleusis and Mithraism in Christianity, cf. Steiner's comments in From Jesus to Christ, London 1973, pp.196–200: the conception of Christ as fusing both Dionysus and Mithras. Hyam Maccoby forcefully summarizes the analogies between the eucharist and the Mystery communions: Paul and Hellenism, London 1991, see especially his note, pp.195f. He is probably wrong, however, to distance Paul from Judaism because of the analogies. The Mithraic contacts of early Christianity are shown in a new light by the Gospel of Philip discovered at Nag Hammadi, which bases Christian life around a highly sacramental order of initiation through several stages: see further Welburn, A., Beginnings of Christianity, especially pp.176–80.

15a. The materials have more recently been subject to fascinating re-examination by Z.P. Thundy, Buddha and Christ, Leiden and New York, 1993. The chief legendary account of the Buddha's life, which Seydel compares with the Gospels, is the Buddhacarita by the first-century Indian poet Ashvagosha (available in the Sacred Books of the East series, vol. XLIX, Delhi 1965. For more on the spiritual background of the parallel legends of Simeon and Asita, see R. Steiner, *The Gospel of Luke*, London 1964, pp.54ff.

15b. For initiation-stages in the Gospels, see R. Steiner, *The Gospel of St John*, New York 1962, pp.170–73. That is not to say that Christ requires instruction and further spiritual training — a misunderstanding that Steiner sought to correct in *Man in the Light of Occultism, Theosophy and Philosophy*, London 1964, pp.155f. Steiner identified one source of the 'typical pattern' of the Christ-initiate's life in an Essene writing from the first century BC: *Esoteric Christianity*, London 1984, p.114. For the possibility that this is the Essene *Community Rule*, see Welburn, A., *Beginnings of Christianity*, p.309n10. Another pre-Christian Mystery-prototype which was preserved and adapted by early Christianity is evidently that which underlies the Apocalypse, or Book of Revelation: see p.114 below.

16. The New Testament 'Second Letter of Peter' uses explicit Mystery-language, calling the disciples who witnessed the Transfiguration *epoptai* — the term for participants in the Great Mysteries at Eleusis (2 Peter 1, 16). The author of the Letter evidently came from a Hellenistic background and was familiar with the Mysteries. He recognized in the events of the Christian tradition the inner reality which Steiner describes. Yet he stands at the same time in the mainstream of the early Church, giving literary form to the traditions in the name of Peter, the acknowledged head of the Twelve disciples or original Community.

17. John 1, 11.

18. John 1, 1 and 3.

19. Augustine, *Contra epistolam Manichaei quam vocant fundamenti*, 6.

20. The terms used were *theothenai, apotheosis*, etc. from the root *theos* ('God').

21. Matthew 23, 20.

22. See the evidence assembled by Schmithals, W., *Gnosticism in Corinth*, New York 1971, pp.52ff, for the 'pre-Christian Christ myth,' connected with the experience of union with a spiritual or primordial Christ in various Jewish and Gnostic sources. Schmithals stresses that this Christ-figure, who becomes known through an inner process of union, cannot be explained from the Church's conception of a Christ who appears incarnate in the world. One important text in this tradition is presented and discussed also in Welburn, A., *Gnosis, the Mysteries and Christianity*, Edinburgh 1994, pp.149ff. The experience is there characterized as 'becoming an image,' i.e. being merged into a supersensible vision. The Christ-initiation, independent of any relation to the historical Christ, was preserved in various Gnostic sects.

For the Gnostics as continuing older initiation-practices, see R. Steiner, *Christianity as Mystical Fact*, London 1972, p.132.

23. This is what Steiner often calls by the name of 'esoteric Christianity.' It is not in any simple sense a matter of 'secret doctrines,' but of an inner process and a changed relationship to the contents of Christianity. Cf. below p.137.

Rudolf Steiner spoke about the Gospels and other aspects of early Christianity from this 'esoteric' perspective in numerous lectures and books (cf. Suggestions for Further Reading at the end of this volume).

6. The Apocalypse of John

1. Apocalypse 1, 1. The author of the Apocalypse specifically calls himself John. Church tradition identified him with the apostle John, brother of James and one of the Twelve. Church tradition rather belatedly also identified John brother of James as the writer of the Fourth Gospel, who in the Gospel itself identifies himself only as 'the Disciple whom Jesus loved.' None of these identifications is obvious. Rudolf Steiner showed that the phrase in the Fourth Gospel actually refers to the initiate Lazarus, whose Mystery 'death and resurrection' stands in the very centre of the Gospel (see R. Steiner, *The Gospel of St John*, New York 1973.) More recently a very similar case has been argued by F. Filson, the well-known New Testament scholar. Below, Steiner goes on to identify the writer of the Apocalypse with 'the Disciple whom Jesus loved' — and so with the first Christian initiate. However, it is notable that in later lectures Steiner referred merely to 'the Apocalyptist' and to the 'legendary' associations of the figure of John.

2. Apocalypse 1, 10f. See further note 35 below.

3. Rudolf Steiner works out this insight with great consistency and detail in his approach to the Apocalypse. We cannot translate its images ('signs') until we understand the inner process which the seer undergoes. With regard to the time-scheme of the prophecies, for example, we cannot orientate ourselves unless we realize that the seer's awakening to higher knowledge leads to an expansion of vision, both forward into the future and back to the beginning, the primal source of the Christian revelation. Once we do grasp this, moreover, the Apocalypse ceases to seem an irrational sequence of unrelated images: the sudden transitions correspond to moments of inner breakthrough in the life of the soul undergoing initiation, a consistent if sometimes dramatic spiritual development; and the meaning of future events emerges, not as an arbitrary irruption into the present consciousness of the seer, but as the completion of a pattern, a grand design that has been unfolding in past history — as the fulfilment, in short, of an imaginative whole. Cf. above, Chapter 2, note 14.

4. Apocalypse 2, 1–7.
5. An account of them is given by the heresiologist Irenaeus, *Against Heresies* I, 26, 3.
6. An early Christian text *On True Belief* makes this clear. It points out the contrast with mere dogmatic belief, and insists for example that 'the testimonies of pagan wise men must not be thrown away,' i.e. the wisdom of the Mysteries. Its author refers to what he calls 'the generous nature of theosophy' — 'divine wisdom': 'a word which was itself,' comments Robin Lane Fox, 'a Christian coinage. It stood for the "wisdom of God" as opposed to the wisdom of mere philosophers' (see Lane Fox, R., *Pagans and Christians*, Harmondsworth 1986, p.680).
7. Each of the Communities addressed stands therefore for a certain approach to the divine, under the guidance of a special Spirit. We learn later that each of these Spirits was especially prevalent in a particular age of history (an idea already met in the Jewish apocalypses such as the Book of Enoch, etc.). For the sequence of times, see below (especially note 35). The Communities are chosen, therefore, because in them something from the past has survived or something from the future is anticipated; between them, they represent the whole course of human history and man's changing relationship to the divine.

   Cf. R. Steiner, *Reading the Pictures from the Apocalypse*, New York 1993, pp.76–78.
8. For the use of pre-Christian Mystery descriptions, seen as fulfilled in Christ, cf. above p.104 and note.

   Steiner's radical departure here from other theories of the book's origin has much to recommend it. For example, the description of the birth of the Messiah in 12, 5 has proved difficult to see as an imaginative reworking of the birth at Bethlehem from the Gospels! In Steiner's view, it is clearly understandable as a Mystery-imagination prior to the physical event.
9. 'What likeness do we see in the Christ of the Apocalypse,' asked Loisy, 'riding on a white horse, with his name of mystery, his eyes of flame, the sword coming out of his mouth, his flashing diadems and mantle red with blood? We see the likeness of a solar deity, of Mithra as he is depicted on horseback in bas-reliefs. In that connection a long story might be told of the Christ of the Apocalypse with his seven Churches, his seven attendant stars, his seven Spirits — he who is the Holy, he who is the True. It is the figure of an astral divinity, presiding over the heavenly spheres, like Mithra, like Attis and many another.' (*The Birth of the Christian Religion*, London 1948, p.225.)
10. Cf. John 21, 22. On the significance of this phrase, see above pp.110f. Steiner identifies the writer of the Apocalypse, who now calls

himself 'John' (1, 1 etc.) with the beloved disciple and witness of the resurrection:

> Although the critics dispute it, he was the author of the Gospel of John, the Apocalypse and of the Letters of John. Throughout his life he had not always said, 'Children, love one another!' (cf. 1 John 3, 11). He had written a work which belongs to the most difficult productions of mankind — the Apocalypse — and the Gospel of John, which penetrates most deeply into the human soul. He had gained the right to pronounce such a saying only through a long life and through what he had accomplished. (R. Steiner, *From Jesus to Christ*, London 1973, pp.99f.)

The critics still dispute: see Kümmel, W.G., *Introduction to the New Testament*, London 1975, pp.469–72. For the recognition of some connections between the Apocalypse and the other 'Johannine' writings see however Cullmann, O., *The Johannine Circle*, London 1976, pp.53f.

11. Steiner spoke about the Mysteries of the Apocalypse in books and lectures throughout his life; see in particular: *The Apocalypse of St John*, London 1977; *Reading the Pictures of the Apocalypse; The Fall of the Spirits of Darkness*, London 1993.

12. That is, the one which came to be included in the accepted collection of writings called the New Testament. The formation of the canon was complex, and controversial. Around AD 175, there was still widespread opposition in the Church to the acceptance of all the writings in the name of John. Some elements continued to favour the *Apocalypse of Peter* over our Revelation; sometimes copies of the scriptures included the apocalyptic visions of the so-called *Shepherd of Hermas* (a Christian prophet of very early post-apostolic times, whose work shows many esoteric and Mystery characteristics). In parts of the Eastern Church, the Revelation of John was still not fully accepted until the ninth century.

13. A fascinating (and sometimes cautionary) history of this exoteric interpretation can be found in Cohn, Norman, *The Pursuit of the Millennium*, London 1970.

    The history of the esoteric or Mystery-interpretation remains to be written.

14. Apocalypse 1, 10.

15. For more detail concerning the levels of spiritual vision which Steiner characterizes below, see his *Stages of Higher Knowledge*, New York 1981.

16. Apocalypse 1, 13f.

17. Apocalypse 1, 20.

18. Apocalypse 1, 16.

19. Apocalypse 1, 20.

20. Apocalypse 1, 16.

21. Apocalypse 1, 17.

22. Apocalypse 1, 18. Christ identifies himself with the undying, the 'Alpha and Omega,' beginning and end or Eternal, and so master over time. E. Norden notes that Christ is presented here as the *Aion*: 'For "Beginning and End" is nothing but a description of *Aion* — an ancient, widespread formula of the Aion Mysteries' *(Die Geburt des Kindes*, Darmstadt 1969, p.50). The concept of the Eternal *(Aion*, unageing Chronos, etc.) belongs to the Mystery-doctrine of Orphism and the other parallel cults (see above Chapter 3, note 1). The Orphic initiate was transformed into Chronos who 'was represented we are told, as a winged serpent with additional heads of a bull and a lion, and between them the face of a god ... Chronos' lion and bull heads are most naturally understood as pictorial expressions of the concepts of "all-mastering" and "tireless" Time that we find in fifth-century poetry.' (West, M.L., *The Orphic Poems*, Oxford 1983, pp.191f.) He notes the parallel in Ezekiel 1, 6–10. Compare also the animal forms of the Living Creatures attending upon the *Aion*-Christ. Chronos' body was a winged serpent, cf. eagle in the Living Creatures.

23. Apocalypse 4, 1.

24. Apocalypse 4, 2; 6.

25. 'Before the prophetic vision of the seer John comes to the point of revealing the laws and secrets of the future ... it plunges retrospectively into the very beginning of evolution. It is only from this retrospect that the prophetic pre-vision is brought forth. We might regard the fourth and fifth chapters of the Apocalypse as ... a New Testament Genesis. Here the picture of the "sea of glass" may serve as a key. We witness a definite moment in the evolution of the world. Aeons of evolution have already run their course in the spiritual sphere. Now comes the first germination of physical, corporeal existence.' (Bock, Emil *The Apocalypse*, London 1957, p.44.)

26. Apocalypse 4, 4.

27. Apocalypse 4, 6–8. *Aion* formula once more at the end. 'One might be inclined to interpret the circles and figures in Chapter 4 astronomically. Could not the ring of twenty-four Elders round the Throne reflect the twelve signs of the zodiac? Do not the seven spiritual lights point to the seven planets? ... Even the figures of the Four Living Creatures may be found again in the sky: they are the constellations of the Lion, the Bull, the Water-carrier, and the Scorpion (the Scorpion appears as the counterpart of the Eagle), which form the great cross of the zodiac ... However, a reference to the constellations of the starry sky is not a sufficient explanation of the apocalyptic symbols. The starlit heaven itself is just another Apocalypse, which in its picture alphabet corresponds in a sense to the Apocalypse of John. The one book can illumine the other, but it cannot explain it.' (Bock, Emil *The Apocalypse*, London 1957, p.43.)

28. Apocalyse 5, 5.
29. Philo, *De specialibus legibus* I, 47.
30. Apocalypse 5, 9f.
31. The language of 'universal' or 'catholic' powers is drawn from astrology. 'With earthly *genii* or *daimons,* who protected definite spots, were contrasted the celestial gods, who are "catholic". This word, which was to have such a great destiny, was at first merely an astrological term: it denoted activities which are not limited to individuals, nor to particular events, but apply to the whole human race and to the entire earth': so Cumont, Franz, *Astrology and Religion among the Greeks and Romans,* New York 1960, p.63.
32. Apocalypse 6, 6. 'At this juncture,' comments Steiner, 'there is added to the picture a symbol of something higher, seeming to fill the entire world. For those who go through the initiation of John is added to the symbolism of the ancient initiation a clairvoyant vision: the Priest-King with the golden sash and with feet that seem to be cast metal, his head covered in hair that is white like wool, in his mouth a fiery sword and in his hand the seven cosmic stars (Saturn, Sun, Moon, Mars, Mercury, Jupiter and Venus). This form which appears in the centre was represented in the archaic initiations only as the fifth of the animal-forms. It had only germinal existence in ancient humanity. It emerges as the Son of Man who rules the seven stars only later when he reveals to man his true form.' (*Apocalypse of St John,* pp.54f.) Apocalypse 1, 12.
33. Apocalypse 7, 4.
34. Apocalypse 8, 7.
35. The communities of the Seven Letters represent ages of human history, for which Rudolf Steiner gave dates as follows, based upon the cosmic rhythm of the precession of the equinoxes:

Ephesus	Smyrna	Pergamum	Thyatira	Sardis	Philadelphia	Laodicea
7227	5067	2907	747 BC	AD 415	3575	5735	7895

BC   Christ-event   AD

On the significance of these periods ('cultural epochs'), see R. Steiner, *The Gospel of St John,* pp.128–36.

All these ages fall within the fifth of the larger periods represented by the angels with the Trumpets. The level of spiritual perception connected with the latter thus opens out the vista into the primordial past as well as the distant future.
36. Apocalypse 10, 9.
37. Apocalypse 11, 8.
38. Apocalypse 11, 15.
39. Apocalypse 11, 19.
40. Apocalypse 10, 1f.

41. Apocalypse 10, 9f.

42. Corresponding on the plane of the Seven Letters to 'the community at Thyatira. Here Christ announces himself as the "Son of God" who has "eyes like flames of fire and feet like brass". He announces himself now as the Son of God. He is now the leader of a fourth age of civilization, when humanity has descended to the physical plane, when man has set his own stamp upon the external world. The period has now come when the Deity himself becomes man, becomes flesh, becomes a person.' *(The Apocalypse of St John,* p.70.) For the chronology of the ages represented by the Seven Letters, see note 35 above.

43. Apocalypse 12, 1–39. (Quotation added.)

44. Cf. Apocalypse 12, 5: 'Her child was caught up to God and to his Throne.'

45. Apocalypse 12, 9. Adela Yarbro-Collins shows that the narrative of the Woman and the Dragon derives from the myth of the Greek goddess Leto, her sun-child Apollo and the dragon or Python at Delphi — the site of Apollo's oracle. She also sees the influence of the figure of Isis combined with that of Leto, confirming Steiner's reference to the myth of Osiris: *The Combat Myth in the Book of Revelation,* Missoula 1976, pp.56–71, 245–70. On the myth of the Python, see R. Steiner, *Christ and the Spiritual World and the Search for the Holy Grail,* London 1963, pp.64–71. Steiner refers the myth to a cosmic event, seen as a part of the preparation for the Christ-Event on earth (cf. above, Chapter 6, note 8).

    In the myth, Apollo gained knowledge (like many a legendary dragon-slayer) from the serpent's blood. Divine knowledge is brought to earth through the medium of the Pythia, who speaks the oracles of the god as his priestess. The Jewish apocalypses which preceded and were contemporaneous with that of John also see divine knowledge brought down to earth — but evaluate it differently: as a source of human temptation. The Essene movement in particular, argues Martin Hengel, rejected such wisdom as 'demonic knowledge coming from the betrayal of divine secrets (I Enoch 16, 3) by the fallen angels, and it may be supposed that in effect this included all the wisdom of the pagans and the refined culture of the Hellenistic period.' *(Judaism and Hellenism,* London 1974, I, p.243.) He also compares (p.190) the myth of Prometheus, cf. above p.37. The Christian apocalyptist seems more ambiguous than either: such knowledge is dangerous, but can be redeemed through the new Christ-Mystery.

46. See Apocalypse 13, 18. The 'Roman history' interpretation of the Apocalypse of which this identification usually forms part has many initially attractive features. It suggests that John is pitting the power of his spiritual vision against the worldly power of the Roman state

which persecuted the Church. A precise, and rather dramatic situation is thus projected, enabling us to 'place' the Apocalypse in Christian history. It seems at first, also, to make everything extremely clear: 'All we need,' comments G.B. Caird, 'is a list of the Roman emperors, and a little elementary computation ... But difficulties soon multiply. With which emperor are we to start counting, Julius, Augustus, or perhaps Caligula, in whom the monster's tendencies first made their appearance? Are we to count all the emperors or only those who were deified by an act of the Senate ...? ... Since our problems are not due to any lack of historical information, there is no reason to think that John's first-century readers would have been in any better case than we are. It is probable, therefore, that we have been looking for the wrong sort of solution.' Caird, G.B., *The Revelation of St John the Divine*, London 1966, pp.217f. Cf. also his discussion pp.174–76.

47. In *Reading the Pictures of the Apocalypse*, p.20, Steiner gives the sign of the Christ as the Sun-Intelligence as follows:

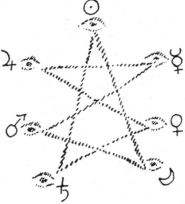

'This is at the same time,' he adds, 'the occult sign of the Lamb ... In occult schools, the signs of the seven planets are written next to the seven eyes. The seven eyes signify nothing other than the seven planets, while the names of the planets designate the spirits incarnated in them (their Intelligence). "Saturn" is the name of the soul of Saturn. The names of the planets come from the spirits of the seven planets found around our earth, influencing human life. The Lamb, Christ, contains all seven. Christ is the Alpha and Omega, and the seven planets are related to him as members to the whole body ... Christ is regent of all these world spheres. Their actions make up only part of his being: he unites them all.' (pp.20f)

   Similar ideas in other early Christian literature, notably in the name of John — such as the Gnostic *Secret Book of John* — are discussed by Welburn, A., *Beginnings of Christianity*, Edinburgh 1991, pp.277ff.

48. Apocalypse 13, 11.

49. See further Steiner's comments in *Michaelmas and the Soul-Forces of Man*, New York 1982, pp.6ff.

50. 'The power by which the spirit of the Sun overcomes and casts into the abyss is called the "Countenance" of the Sun-spirit. The Countenance of the Sun-spirit is Michael. Standing for the Sun-spirit, so to speak, he conquers the two-horned Beast who leads men astray, the great dragon. This is presented to the seer in the image of Michael with the key to the abyss and the chain in his hand. IIe stands before God and holds the hostile forces captive in chains.' (R. Steiner, *The Apocalypse of St John*, p.203.)

Steiner points out that this image meets us already in the ancient Babylonian Mysteries, as Marduk confronting Tiamat, the Dragon, in the *Enuma Elish* (above, Chapter 1, note 10). Towards the end of his life, Steiner spoke increasingly about the importance of the Michael-Imagination and the transformation it must undergo. See *The Mission of the Archangel Michael*, New York 1961; also the studies on the Michael-Mystery in *Anthroposophical Leading Thoughts*, London 1973.

51. Apocalypse 21, 2f. (Quotation added.)

52. Gospel of John 20, 29.

53. Apocalypse 21, 22f.

54. Apocalypse 22, 10. Cf. p.79 above.

7. *The Rediscovery of the Cosmic Christ*

1. See on this Welburn, A., *The Beginnings of Christianity*, Edinburgh 1991, pp.100ff. In Alexandria, one of the three great centres of early Christianity alongside Antioch and Rome, the cosmic meaning of the birth of Christ at the baptism remained for centuries the dominant idea. Roman traditions about the birth of Jesus only gradually displaced this conception, and replaced the festival with our 'Christmas,' gradually establishing this custom throughout the Church. The *Gospel of Philip*, rediscovered since Rudolf Steiner's time, shows similar conceptions prevailing in early Antioch. Its Saying 81 reads: 'Jesus revealed [in the] Jordan the *pleroma* of the kingdom of heaven. He who came into being before the All was begotten again. He who was anointed at first was anointed again, he who was redeemed redeemed again.' Rudolf Steiner referred to the reading of the 'Western text' of the New Testament (an early and authoritative branch of the manuscripts), which gives the oracle of the heavenly voice at Jesus' baptism in the form 'You are my beloved Son, this day I have begotten you': see R. Steiner, *The Gospel of Matthew*, London 1965, p.127. On the Mystery-background of the January 6 festival, see further R. Steiner, *The Festivals and their Meaning*, London

1981, pp.88f; cf. the fascinating information in Norden, E., *Die Geburt des Kindes*, Darmstadt 1969, pp.33ff.

2. That is, the Christ-impulse of which Rudolf Steiner often spoke. Our task nowadays is to become conscious of the workings of this impulse, and so to find once again its cosmic, wider significance for ourselves and our whole environment. He emphasised:

> how we can come again to the wisdom which once lived in men instinctively and remained, to the extent that at the time of the Mystery of Golgotha there were still some who knew how to celebrate the epiphany of the Christ-being. We in our day must achieve understanding of the Christ as a cosmic being — a cosmic being who united himself with the earth. The time at which this understanding becomes accessible to the greater part of mankind upon earth, is the time of the cosmic 'holy night' whose advent we await. *(Festivals and their Meaning, p.108.)*

See further R. Steiner, *The Christ-Impulse and the Development of Ego-Consciousness*, New York 1976.

3. This wisdom was expressed above all in the Gnostic movement, which modern discoveries such as the Gnostic library from Nag Hammadi have confirmed played a crucial role in the development of the Gospel tradition and Christian thought up to the fourth century. 'The term Gnostics,' Steiner explained, 'is applied to all those writers from the first centuries of Christianity who sought for a deeper, spiritual meaning in its teachings ... They are to be understood as thinkers steeped in the ancient mysteriosophy and striving to comprehend Christianity from the viewpoint of the Mysteries': *Christianity as Mystical Fact*, London 1972, p.132. A good survey of the new discoveries and the role of Gnosticism is Rudolph, K. *Gnosis*, Edinburgh 1984. Steiner saw that it was imperative to understand the ancient wisdom in relation to Christianity; he was equally clear that it could not and should not be revived in the same form today, since that would be to miss the uniquely Christian transformation of the ancient knowledge. Anthroposophy must begin precisely with that transformation and find a modern way to spiritual understanding. See especially R. Steiner, *Anthroposophical Leading Thoughts*, London 1973, pp.175ff.

4. The several tribes of Huns, Goths, Visigoths, and so on, who migrated across Europe in the fourth century caused widespread confusion and devastation, though many of them were partly Romanized and even Christian. Alaric with his Goths sacked Rome early in the next century (AD 410) but rapidly reached an accommodation with the imperial administration. The destabilizing effect, however, was profound.

5. The 'two natures' theology was developed in Antioch in the early

centuries; later it was displaced by the Western theology which put the stress on the birth, the earthly 'becoming human' of the Christ.

6. The shift to the emotional is most readily seen in Augustine, who lived through the changes of the late fourth century and effectively shaped the Christianity of the Middle Ages. Steiner described him as having a 'passionate nature' with correspondingly 'deep spiritual needs,' *Christianity as Mystical Fact*, p.145. On the way in which love takes over from the older wisdom in the life and thought of Augustine, see the brilliantly readable biography by Peter Brown, *Augustine of Hippo*, London 1969, especially pp.154ff, 257ff, etc.

   After Augustine's time, the great Alexandrian theologies based on *gnosis* and cosmic in scope, most notably synthesised in the thought of Origen, were decisively rejected by the Church.

7. Rudolf Steiner drew attention particularly to the beautiful nativity plays from Oberufer which had been rediscovered by his one-time mentor, the philosopher Karl Julius Schroer. They are often performed in Steiner schools and other institutions: see Harwood, A.C. (trans.), *Christmas Plays from Oberufer*, Bristol 1993.

8. The *Legenda Aurea* of Jacobus of Voragine is a mediaeval cycle of saint- and miracle-stories, preserving some material of very ancient date. Rudolf Steiner frequently discussed it, e.g. in *The Temple Legend*, London 1985. The legend to which he here refers and many similar ideas are collected and described in Rahner, Hugo, *Greek Myth and Christian Mystery*, London 1963, pp.61ff. Steiner regarded the adoption of the Christmas-tree symbol as in the right spirit, though he was quite aware that it is a very recent feature of Christmas celebrations, going back only to the nineteenth century (R. Steiner, *Festivals and their Meaning*, p.30).

9. Such a conception is summed up e.g. in the work by Eusebius of Caesarea, *The Preparation for the Gospel (Praeparatio Evangelica)*.

10. Emil Bock developed this contrast in his *Cäsaren und Apostel (Caesars and Apostles)* Stuttgart 1978.

   W. Schneemelcher collects some evidence about the Roman cult, including that which shows that:

> 'gospel' was an important sacral word in the Imperial cult ... And not only the news of the monarch's birth but also the stories of the further course of his life are given the same designation. In particular the news of the enthronement of the 'saviour' [i.e. the Emperor] was a gospel. Here it is precisely the conceptions of 'saviour' and 'glad tidings' (gospel) which belong closely together. (in Hennecke, E. and Schneemelcher, W., *New Testament Apocrypha*, vol. I, London 1963 p.72.)

He quotes G. Friedrich: 'The Imperial cult and the Bible have this in common that for them the enthronement, which leads on a new time and gives peace to the world, is a gospel for mankind.' Schneemel-cher also admits that 'the differences must not of course be over-looked.' The Roman Emperors inherited their role as divine rulers and saviours of their people via the successors of Alexander the Great from the ancient Near East over which they successively ruled. The Pharaohs of Egypt and the sacral kings of Babylon obtained their power from the Mysteries, and were identified in essence with the cosmic order established at creation. The Pharaoh 'sat on the throne of Atum,' that is, the primordial God. In the New Year festival at Babylon the king took part in Mystery-rites where he played the part of the creator-god Marduk in his victory over chaos. The Roman Emperors still maintained their link with the Mysteries, though their pursuit of power became increasingly corrupt: see R. Steiner, *Building Stones for an Understanding of the Mystery of Golgotha*, London 1972, pp.115ff.

11. The acceptance of this fact in early Christian circles is now affirmed by the *Gospel of Thomas* and the *Gospel of Philip* found in the Nag Hammadi library. See *Gospel of Thomas* 19: 'Jesus said: Blessed is he who was before he came into being ...' The one who knows his eternal self in this way, it continues, 'shall not taste death.' The *Gospel of Philip* 57 quotes the same Saying of the Lord and explains: 'For he who is came into being and will be.'

12. Paul, 1 Corinthians 15, 13f.

13. I have added the Latin, which Steiner frequently quotes elsewhere. The three formulae were much used in the Rosicrucian meditative path which has carried on Christian esotericism into modern times; cf. R. Steiner, *Esoteric Christianity and the Mission of Christian Rosen-creutz*, London 1984. They have clear prototypes however, for example in the *Gospel of Philip* — see Sayings 74, 96 and 109.

14. That is, as the *Logos*, the divine Reason expressed in the world and born from the mind of God: see above, pp.81ff.

15'. The content of the archaic mysteriosophy emerged, through Christianity, to become an historical event; and in this sense Christianity is not only the fulfilment of the hopes expressed by the prophets of Jewish tradition, but also of what had been prefigured in the Mysteries. The cross on Golgotha is the Mystery-cult of antiquity epitomized in an historical fact.' (R. Steiner, *Christianity as Mystical Fact*, p.143.)

16. Cf. above Chapter 5, note 7.

17. Above, pp.99ff.

18. For an expression in early Christianity of the struggle to replace the blood-forces with those of Christ, see J. Daniélou, *The Origins of Latin Christianity*, London 1977, pp.75ff, quoting the interesting and esoteric text *On the Threefold Fruits of Christian Life*.

Further Reading

The list does not include editions of primary texts, but books and in some cases collections of sources in translation relevant to the approach of this volume.

Angus, S. *The Mystery Religions and Christianity*. With a new Foreword by T.H. Gaster, New York 1966.

Bock, E. *The Apocalypse of St John*. Edinburgh 1980.

Burkert, W. *Ancient Mystery Cults*. London 1987.

——, *Lore and Science in ancient Pythagoreanism*. Harvard 1972.

Campbell, J. (ed.) *The Mysteries. Papers from ERANOS*. Princeton 1971.

Cumont, F. *Astrology among the Greeks and Romans*. New York 1960.

——, *Oriental Religions in Roman Paganism*. New York 1956.

Dodds, E.R. *The Greeks and the Irrational*. Berkeley, Los Angeles and London 1951.

Eliade, M. *History of Religious Ideas*. London 1979.

——, *Rites and Symbols of Initiation*. New York 1965.

Frieling, R. *Christianity and Reincarnation*. Edinburgh 1977.

——, *Hidden Treasures in the Psalms*. London 1967.

Goodenough, E.R. *Jewish Symbols of the Graeco-Roman Period*. (Shorter ed.) Princeton 1988.

Godwin, J. *Music, Mysticism and Magic*. London and New York 1987.

Hadas, M. *Hellenistic Culture*. New York 1972.

Heidenreich, A. *The Book of Revelation*. Edinburgh 1977.

——, *Healings in the Gospels*. Edinburgh 1980.

——, *The Unknown in the Gospels*. London 1972.

Jung, C.G. and Kerenyi, K. *Essays on a Science of Mythology. The Myth of the Divine Child and the Mysteries of Eleusis*. Princeton 1965.

Lievegood, B.C.J. *Mystery Streams in Europe and the New Mysteries*. New York 1982.

Martin, L. *Hellenistic Religions*. Oxford 1987.

Meyer, M. *The Ancient Mysteries. A Sourcebook*. New York 1987.

Morgan, M.L. *Platonic Piety. Philosophy and Ritual in Fourth Century Athens*. New Haven and London 1990.

Nock, A.D. *Conversion*. Oxford 1961.

Prokofieff, S. *Rudolf Steiner and the Founding of the New Mysteries*. London 1986.

Quispel, G. *The Secret Book of Revelation*. London 1979.

Ringgren, H. *The Faith of Qumran*. New York 1995.

Rudolph, K. *Gnosticism*. Edinburgh 1984.

Snell, B. *The Discovery of the Mind*. New York 1982.

Steiner, R. *The Apocalypse of John*. London 1977.

——, *Building Stones for an Understanding of the Mystery of Golgotha*. London 1972.

——, *Christianity as Mystical Fact*. London 1972.

——, *The Easter Festival in relation to the Mysteries*. London 1968.

——, *Egyptian Myths and Mysteries*. New York 1971.

——, *Mysteries of the East and Christianity*. London 1972.

——, *Wonders of the World, Ordeals of the Soul, Revelations of the Spirit*. London 1963.

Thundy, Z.P. *Buddha and Christ*. Leiden and New York 1993.

Wegman, I. *The Mysteries*. London 1995.

Welburn, A.J. *The Beginnings of Christianity*. Edinburgh 1991.

West, M.L. *Early Greek Philosophy and the Orient*. Oxford 1971.

——, *The Orphic Poems*. Oxford 1983.